INNOVATE!

Mark O'Hare

INNOVATE!

How to
Gain and Sustain
Competitive Advantage

BASIL BLACKWELL

First published 1988

Basil Blackwell Ltd
108 Cowley Road, Oxford, OX4 1JF, UK

Basil Blackwell Inc.
432 Park Avenue South, Suite 1503
New York, NY 10016, USA

British Library Cataloguing in Publication Data

O'Hare, Mark
  Innovate!: how to gain and sustain
  competitive advantage.
  1. Business firms. Innovation. Management
  I. Title
  658.4'063
  ISBN–0–631–16448–0

Library of Congress Cataloging in Publication Data

O'Hare, Mark.
  Innovate!: how to gain and sustain competitive
  advantage.
  1. Creative ability in business. 2. Organizational
  effectiveness. I. Title
  HD53.037   1988   658.4'094   88–22330
  ISBN 0–631–16448–0

Typeset in 10½ on 12 pt Plantin
by Opus, Oxford
Printed in Great Britain by Billing and Sons Ltd, Worcester

CONTENTS

ACKNOWLEDGEMENTS

This is a practical book, written for practising managers. Its objective is straightforward: to help its readers meet one of today's most pressing management challenges – that of making their own businesses more innovative. It draws on several years' experience of advising innovative companies of all sizes from a wide range of industries.

Being a practical book, it relies heavily on the experiences of many firms, managers and entrepreneurs. They are too numerous to mention. I am particularly indebted to Adrian Beecroft of Alan Patricof Associates, Timothy Breene of the WCRS Group, Tom Farmer of Kwik-Fit, Ron Lander of Scotlander, Maurice Pinto, Philippe Le Roux of Norton Villiers Triumph and Eddy Shah of Messenger Group. Torbjorn Bjurgert of Procede made a major contribution to developing the material for Chapter 14, Adaptive and Repetitive Behaviour. Without their participation and efforts, this book would not have been possible.

I am particularly grateful to Anthony Simonds-Gooding, Chief Executive of British Satellite Broadcasting. His breadth of innovative experience and perceptive critical assistance have been invaluable. Tim Goodfellow of publishers Basil Blackwell made valuable constructive inputs throughout the period of writing, both as regards the book's content and its structure.

Needless to say, this book also required enormous secretarial assistance. Sophy Brewer and Alison Hill did a tremendous job taking the original handwritten manuscript through several iterations to reach the final draft. That they did this on top of an already hectic work schedule and remained cheerful and enthusiastic throughout is a remarkable feat. Thank you. They were helped in the task by Susy Pash,. who also deserves my fullest praise and thanks.

There is another kind of support that was crucial to the successful completion of this book. It was written during evenings, weekends and holidays. My wife Lindy and daughters Cordelia and Josephine learned what it was like to be without a husband and father. Lindy made a special contribution by supporting the book when we were all tired of it. Her love and encouragement were absolutely essential. Without them the book would not have been written. For that reason the book is dedicated, with love and gratitude, to her.

FOREWORD by Anthony Simonds-Gooding

As a prelude to reading this book, I took myself down my own memory lane of some thirty years in business just to assess how much innovation I had encountered. My purpose was to check these experiences against the book.

My first brush with innovation was in the product development department at Birds Eye Foods in the sixties. We spent most of our time producing what we called range extensions – a seventh flavour of mousse; a new type of crumb on the fish; a cut bean to join the sliced one; hake to add to cod and haddock; and so on. One got marks for effort, but in fact we hardly moved the business on, nor were we addressing the fundamentally changing environment that was suddenly surrounding us. In truth, we were tinkering, while Rome burned.

Later, in advertising, working on Lever business, I found myself at the receiving end of some radical product development. It was the launch of Ariel by Proctor and Gamble. Everything about it was wrong, so we convinced ourselves. The product was rooted in the past (soaking, enzymes, old hat); the name was difficult and certainly wrong for a detergent; the pack design was scientific, soft, without impact; the retail price was too high for volume sales; the marketing budget was so huge, P&G could never make a return. So we all thought. How wrong we were. Here was an example of truly bold product development and marketing. When one examined the individual parts, they did not seem to make any sense, but when taken as an integrated whole and applied to the market with total conviction they were irresistible.

When I returned to Birds Eye, it was to a troubled company. After fifteen years of dazzling and uninterrupted success, it was encountering serious market resistance for the first time.

I remember reflecting on the different ways Birds Eye and Levers faced adversity. Levers regarded business as a chess game – cool; analytical; playing strategies, rather than just making moves. As the going got hotter, so Levers became cooler, and quietly set about preparing counter-attacks that would take many years to complete. Birds Eye on the other hand was in total contrast. Brought up in a pioneering culture, based on energy, enthusiasm and improvisation, when things became suddenly difficult the qualities required to cope were not easily at hand. Essentially the reaction was to do what had always been done even more energetically and more enthusiastically.

I was assigned to the task of assessing the external problems and finding strategic solutions. My team consisted of Advertising, Finance and Production, to achieve a broad, business solution rather than a functional or sectoral one; an imaginative approach at that time.

Birds Eye for fifteen years had pioneered the development of the frozen food market. Its market share was totally dominant, over 70 per cent, achieved by a strategy called 'cabinet domination'. With small, in-shop cabinets the cost of delivery was high. The only way to be viable was to ensure high weight-per-drop, which in turned filled out the cabinet, which in turn ensured that the competitor would have no chance of making a similarly viable weight-per-drop.

To make this strategy work Birds Eye had to do a number of things. It had to manufacture the full product range from peas through kippers to chocolate eclairs. Its factories became jacks-of-all-trades. Secondly, the pack sizes needed to be smaller (and consequently expensive) in order to fit a wide range of products into a small freezer space. Thirdly, most of the company's resources went into distribution and high pressure selling.

This strategy worked in an exemplary way until the advent of the supermarket and the home freezer shop. Suddenly the theory of cabinet domination, exploiting small numbers of customers buying from large numbers of small cabinets was turned on its head. Now large numbers of people were coming to a smaller number of very large cabinets to make their purchases.

For Birds Eye it threatened all that the company stood for. It was impossible to dominate cabinets of that size. Competitors with a narrow range of products could now achieve a viable weight-per-drop given the enlarged market. Specialization in manufacturing with higher quality and lower costs became viable. The jack-of-all-trades manufacturer was dying the death of a thousand well-aimed cuts. Similarly, small packets at high prices were overtaken by large packets at low prices.

This analysis was my first experience of a strategic business review, examining the external rather than just the internal influences on the company.

I subsequently went to Whitbread, a company at that time virtually dependent on beer and on the UK market, employing some 40,000 people. It was organized on a geographic basis through regional barons who were lords of all they surveyed – brewing, wholesaling, retailing, property and so on.

Now, some fifteen years on, the story is very different. 30 per cent of the company is outside the UK. It has diversified away from just beer towards food and drink retailing and towards wines and spirits. Its manpower is probably down by a third, and its organization is by division rather than by geography.

This is a story of innovation through geographic diversification, product diversification and organizational changes. The organization, when it was on a geographic basis with generalists in charge, failed to reach the necessary standard of competitiveness to cope with specialist, focused attack. Hence today's manufacturing, wholesaling, retail and international divisions.

This form of innovation is highly innovative against itself, but not outstandingly innovative against the market place where its offering is still similar to that of the best competitors. This sort of innovation ensures that the company runs fast to maintain its position. It cannot, however, leave the pack behind.

One must always beware of outstanding successes inhibiting further change, and encouraging one to rest on one's laurels. Through the seventies, the lager race was on between the major brewers. Allied Breweries had prospered as the market moved from draught to keg beer; they cleaned up with their famous Double Diamond brand and the 'I'm only here for the beer!' advertising slogan. But this success constrained their actions later. It was much more difficult for them to divert investment from this hugely successful brand towards the inevitable (and highly profitable) consumer march towards lager, than it was for those of us who had comparatively weak keg bitter brands.

Then came Saatchis. A UK company that in fifteen years has come from nowhere to lead the world has to be innovative. But where exactly does the act of innovation lie at Saatchi? It lies in financial deal-making and in acquisition. It also lies in superb PR and using other people's rhetoric to make it Saatchi's own. Global communication and holistic communications are two examples of this. But perhaps the most important ingredient in the Saatchi's mix of innovation is the brothers' sustained act of personal will-power to make their vision become a reality. The added value of this innovation thus far has gone to shareholders and to those individuals from whom they acquired companies. The customer will see the benefit in the long term. Certainly if the theories of power of scale, global communications and one-stop-shopping for services begin to become important to a wider community of clients, Saatchis are best placed to exploit that emerging opportunity.

Finally I come to British Satellite Broadcasting, turning technical innovation to commercial account. By putting a high-powered satellite up, one can broadcast direct to homes, and in cost terms can 'pass' every home in Britain for £10 – rather than £300–£500 per home for cable.

The receiver technology will in time lead to high definition and wide-screen television reception; it enables high volume data transmission, carries encryption and is individually addressable, home by home, allowing, for example, Pay Television, Pay-Per-View Television and Parental Control Systems. This innovative technology will be the key catalyst for change in the UK's broadcasting ecology over the next decade.

This demonstrates the difference between creativity and innovation. Creativity is the business of generating ideas. Innovation is the business of making them happen.

Enough of memory lane. Suffice to say, Mark O'Hare's book covers all my experiences in the general area of innovation – and if it had been under my arm during those thirty years, I would have been greatly helped.

Webster's dictionary tells us that the Latin origins of 'innovate' are all to do with 'renewal'. If innovation means renewal, then there is no subject in the world more crucial to the leaders of any business enterprise. If a business fails to innovate then it grows old and eventually it dies.

Innovation is not an easy thing to sustain. There comes a stage in every enterprise's life when preserving the status quo becomes an overriding temptation. Too often this doom-laden characteristic triumphs, partly because human beings in general prefer the apparent certainties of the status quo to the strain and pain of change, and partly because the ill-effects can take time to emerge and therefore be imperceptible until it is too late.

Mark O'Hare's book tackles this crucial subject from the broad to the narrow, in all its varying forms. His descriptions and his prescriptions are put before one in very direct, practical, implementational terms. He codifies for all of us a subject which for some may be instinctive and easy, but for most is difficult. This book really helps.

Anthony Simonds-Gooding
Chief Executive
British Satellite Broadcasting

INTRODUCTION

An age of certainty in the business world has come to an end. For decades the rules of competition in many industries were clearly laid out. Success depended upon following particular and well-known generic strategies. Experience was the best pointer to the future.

That continuity has now gone. Tomorrow can no longer be assumed to be like yesterday. Fundamental changes are moulding the future of markets worldwide – technological change, regulatory change and change in customers' needs. The pace of this change has quickened. Revolution has taken over where evolution was once the norm.

Businessmen must learn to adapt to the new environment. The formulae which once guaranteed success no longer do so: the competitive ground rules are being rewritten. Most importantly, it is businessmen and managers themselves who are writing the new rules. It is strategic innovation that determines the future: by finding new ways to serve their customers, businessmen can shape the competitive environment.

The chaos is here to stay. There will be no return to the stable environment of yesterday. Fluid environments require responsive, indeed proactive, strategies. Innovation is increasingly becoming the most vital ingredient of strategic success in many markets. Achieving optimal efficiency within the existing structure is no longer enough: managers must be prepared to anticipate change, to respond to change, to thrive on change.

A lot has been said and written about innovation already. Much of it focuses on the technological aspects that lie behind many innovations. Even more of it covers the development of new products and services. Yet innovation is more than this. Innovation is about finding new ways of delivering customer value. It is about building competitive advantage by looking at markets in new ways, by rewriting the rules of competition. It is about strategy.

There is a popular mythology which surrounds innovation. It is about the creative spark of genius, the lone product champion succeeding against all the odds. It is a random, probabilistic event. Some of this is true, much of it is not. More importantly, this picture misses out too much that is of fundamental importance for it to be a useful working model of innovation. For innovation is not so much a random event as a process, a fundamental aspect of how companies are run. Above all, it is manageable: some firms are consistently more innovative than others. They have mastered the skills which will increasingly determine corporate success, separating the winners from the losers. Some of these skills are self-evident, others are counter-intuitive. Managing the innovative process is probabilistic in nature. It is about creating the right environment and shortening the odds on success. The approach which works for one firm and in one situation may fail for another. There are no guarantees, no pat formulae to follow.

Managing for innovation requires different skills to managing in a stable environment. The approaches which worked so well in the past can rapidly become barriers to innovation. Past successes must often be cast aside lest they become impediments to progress. Market leaders are no longer secure in their positions; the innovative battle is more often won by the challenger than by the leader. Yet some leaders remain leaders; increasingly they will be those who have learned how to think like challengers.

Above all, innovation is more than an isolated event. It is a process. The path to successful innovation is long and hard. It starts long before the new business concept is generated, with a recognition of the basic need to develop new ways of delivering value. It ends – insofar as it ever does end – long after the new concept has been proven in the marketplace. It is a fundamental aspect of a company's whole strategy, how it chooses to compete in its market. It therefore cannot be tacked on to the firm's existing approach: it must be integrated into the very fabric of the company.

There are many phases to the process. Barriers can arise at any stage, preventing the firm from innovating. Successful innovators recognize this. They orient their basic approach and strategy to smooth the process, to remove the barriers.

This book examines the innovative process. It analyses the reasons for success and failure in each stage. It is based upon our experience at Goodall Alexander O'Hare & Co in helping firms of all sizes and from a range of industries to innovate successfully. It draws upon a wide sample of case studies of successful – and unsuccessful – innovators. It examines companies which have built their businesses by innovating. It also looks at market leaders who have lost their positions by failing to innovate. Seldom is success or failure the result of one isolated action. Rather, it is the culmination of many aspects of how the firm operates, of its basic patterns of behaviour. Each example can provide several valuable perspectives on different stages in the innovative process. Many of the case studies therefore appear more than once, each time to illustrate a distinct point.

Innovation is iconoclastic. Success requires challenging and overturning accepted truths in order to establish a new vision, a new conceptual map. Almost by definition there can be no simple rules which guarantee success. For tomorrow will not be like yesterday. Experience can help managers to develop new ideas, to point the way forward, but it cannot provide the answer alone. In fact, there are no answers, only questions. Successful innovators are those who ask the awkward questions. What does the customer really need? Why do we operate in the way in which we do? How can we restructure our offering to deliver greater value to our customers? What fundamental changes are required in how we define our business? How will the rules of competition change in our industry?

This book is about these questions. If it can help managers to ask them, it will have served its purpose.

I SETTING THE GROUND RULES

1 THE INNOVATION GAP

Innovation is the most pressing challenge facing business today. Managers increasingly recognize that improving efficiency alone is no longer sufficient to guarantee success. Today's competitive environment demands creative approaches to business situations.

The recognition may be there. The results, however, are not. Innovative performance is actually declining in many industries. There is a growing gap between what is required and what is being achieved. The innovation gap.

1 THE INNOVATION GAP

- Competition

- Commitment to innovation

- Innovative performance

- The innovation gap

COMPETITION

Suddenly, everyone is talking about innovation. In the business press, conferences, business schools and the boardroom, senior managers are dedicating more effort, more attention to making their organizations more innovative. Why?

Competition is the driving force. Markets everywhere are becoming more competitive, more perfect in the economic sense. In consumer and industrial products, basic chemicals and manufacturing, transport, retail, communications and financial services, the competitive pace has quickened. Efficiency alone is insufficient. Creativity is needed. The search for enhanced customer value is intense. Firms must continuously strive to find new ways to deliver that customer value, or they risk being eclipsed by more agile competitors. A number of factors have combined to produce this new competitive environment:

- Improved efficiency in the financial markets has increased the pressure to perform in all industries. The rewards for good performance are greater than ever before. The penalties for failure are more rapid, more severe. The City has shown itself to be prepared to back aggressive, innovative management wherever it finds it. This holds for venture capital as well as for acquisitions, where small innovative firms can find the backing to acquire much larger competitors if they can demonstrate an ability to add value to the business.

- The barriers which have defined the business landscape are being redrawn by deregulation, technological change and, perhaps most important of all, by managers' perceptions and vision. Innovation creates its own opportunities. In some cases, previously separate industries are merging, while in others new divisions are being created. Segmentation and customer focus are the key words. This is perhaps nowhere more obvious than in financial services, where organizations as diverse as building societies and retailers – and everything in between – are all competing for the same customer. But it is also happening in broadcasting, printing and publishing, transportation, professional services, retailing and manufacturing.

- Technological change itself provides a double impetus. On the one hand it creates demand for new products and services while on the the other it offers new opportunities for manufacturing, selling and distributing them.

- Customers' needs are evolving more rapidly and in a more segmented manner than ever before. This holds in the consumer markets, where individuals have greater disposable incomes and are subjected to a constant flow of new ideas through a burgeoning media. (The average US consumer receives some two million advertising messages per year.) It also holds in business markets, where increased competitive pressures are forcing managers continually to reassess their product and service needs.

COMMITMENT TO INNOVATION

Successful firms recognize these trends. They have made innovation a corporate priority at all levels. The words and actions of top management reflect this. Figure 1 shows a dramatic picture of this corporate emphasis on innovation. It shows the top performers in the Business 500 list of UK companies, ranked according to high profitability and growth, together with the worst performers in each sector. (Modesty prohibits the identification of the latter group!) The directors' statements in the annual report were analysed to give them a score which measures how much of the report was devoted to innovation in all its aspects (e.g. 0

means there were no references at all, while 10 implies that 75 per cent or more of the commentary related to innovation).

Figure 1: Innovation – a corporate perspective. References to innovation in annual reports

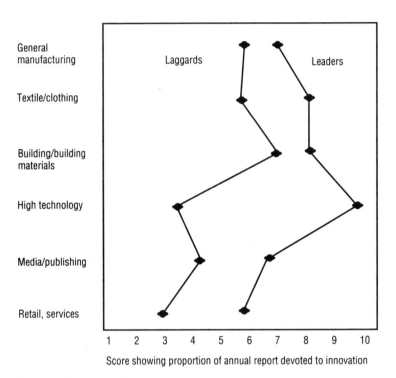

Score showing proportion of annual report devoted to innovation

Source: analysis of annual reports

Several points stand out:

- In every sector the most successful companies have committed themselves to innovation as a higher corporate priority than have the less successful firms. Innovation truly separates the leaders from the laggards.

- This holds in all industries surveyed. Not just in high technology, but in manufacturing, textiles and building materials as well. Innovation is appropriate in every industry. No sectors are excluded.

- The chart admittedly shows what senior management say rather than what they do. However, as every manager knows, public commitment to action at the top of the organization – in particular, from the managing director – is a vital first step to implementing that action. Without it nothing will happen. With it, almost anything is possible.

Finally, which way does the causality run? Does an emphasis on innovation lead to success, or does success allow companies to innovate? The answer is simple . . . both. Successful innovators establish a **virtuous circle** whereby innovation leads to success, providing them with the resources and the will to innovate further. The dominant themes in the leaders' Annual Reports is upbeat – new markets, new products, new challenges. The laggards are – perhaps naturally – too busy restructuring and cutting costs to raise their sights beyond their immediate problems (although innovation is probably the most fundamental long-term issue which many of them face). In which companies will managers be most inclined to search for new ideas, to take risks? Which will be more innovative?

INNOVATIVE PERFORMANCE

If innovation is recognized as an increasingly important factor driving corporate success, the obvious question is: how well are companies meeting the challenge? Are they translating beliefs and statements into actions? How innovative are our companies, large and small?

The answers are less than encouraging. All the evidence suggests that true innovation is becoming increasingly risky and expensive. Figure 2 gives one example. It looks at launches of new food products into UK grocery outlets during the early 1980s. Although the rate at which new products have appeared on the market has remained broadly constant, fewer of them succeed than before. The proportion which are still stocked in a broad range of outlets at a given period after launch declined steadily over the period. Of those launched in 1980, 74 per cent remained on supermarket shelves one year after the launch. Only 14 per cent of those launched in 1986 were still available one year later.

Worse still, of those which survived, only a small proportion have gained a significant market share and, with it, profitability. (To take an even more discouraging example, this time from the US: of approximately 11,000 new food products launched during the 1970s, only 93 –

Figure 2: Survival of new food products

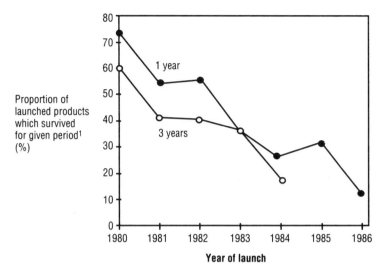

Proportion of launched products which survived for given period[1] (%)

Year of launch

[1]Defined to be those products which appear in Shaw's price list

Source: analysis of UK national food product launches, 1980–1986

that's 0.8 per cent – ever achieved annual sales of $15 million. How many of those will have been profitable?)

Why the failure? Are consumer product companies simply innovating 'less well' than before? Has creativity declined? For the answer we need look no further than one of the key forces driving the innovation process itself: competition. At the same time as increasing the need for innovation, the heightened competitive environment makes it more difficult for innovative new products to succeed. Improved information flows and retail management techniques enable the grocery multiples to spot underperforming products rapidly and to weed them out. There is simply no space on the crowded supermarket shelves of the late 1980s for weak products. Every survey conducted asking consumer products companies what they believe to be the key criteria for new product success indicates the growing importance of **distribution**. 'Me-toos' seldom succeed. Unless a product offers the customer some distinct and tangible benefit, it is unlikely to survive.

In other industries, the traditional approaches adopted by innovators have been left behind by structural changes in the market. The pharmaceuticals industry provides an excellent example. In 1961 93 new drugs were launched worldwide. By 1980 the figure had halved to 48. These figures represent a steady underlying trend. Figure 3 shows how the US drugs industry launched over 40 medicines per year *on average* in the late 1950s. Today the figure is stuck firmly below 20. Worse, the industry's total investment in research over the period has risen six-fold in real terms. In other words, each drug coming on to the market is costing on average over 12 times as much to find and develop as previously.

Figure 3: Pharmaceutical research productivity has declined

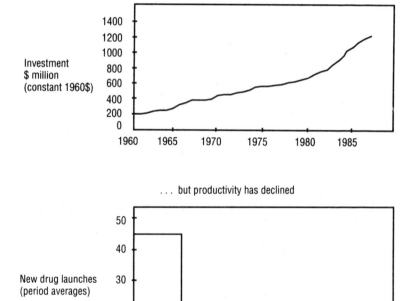

Investment in drug research has increased

... but productivity has declined

Source: **Pharmaceutical Manufacturers Association**

Why the decline? Are there no diseases left to treat? Hardly. The performance of the industry must be viewed in the context of the structural changes which have taken place during the period:

- Controls and regulations designed to limit the risk of a dangerous drug reaching the market have become increasingly strict.

- Governments' desire to contain spiralling health costs have fostered new attitudes to drug prescription and purchasing. While this has reduced the demand for certain drugs, it has also – like every change in market structure – opened new opportunities elsewhere: e.g. drugs which can reduce hospitalization costs are in great demand.

- Patterns of disease worldwide have changed. Incidence of tuberculosis has declined while cancer, heart disease and ulcers have become widespread. New diseases such as AIDS have appeared.

- In many diseases the key criteria for success have changed. Previously the ability to treat the condition at all was of overriding importance. That is often less of an issue today, with several effective remedies available. Convenience of dosage and freedom from side effects are often the most important criteria in a drug's success in the market.

- The approaches available to researchers have changed. In place of the traditional random screening approach (where a huge number of randomly synthesized compounds are tested for their efficacy), today's scientists can understand more fully the disease mechanisms at work. This should help them to tailor new compounds to interfere with a specific stage of the disease process. The whole drug-hunting process can now be made more precise, more targeted.

- New centres of excellence and innovation have developed. From being the exclusive preserve of drugs companies, pharmaceutical research is now carried on in a wider range of foundations, universities and government departments than ever before.

How have pharmaceutical companies responded to these environmental changes? Not very well. Most approach R&D in the same way that they always have done, with large research establishments operating in isolation from marketing or other external inputs. Few fully exploit the new R&D opportunities. In an industry where one discovery can shape a firm's performance for a decade, it is all too easy to see the dearth of new drugs as temporary bad luck rather than as a symptom of something more fundamental. The industry has been slow to explore the underlying reasons for the poor performance. It has therefore been slow to change. (Drugs companies are gradually learning to adapt, however. Some are removing the artificial barriers which had grown between research and other parts of the company, principally marketing departments; making research more responsive to the needs of the market is of vital importance in the new competitive environment. Others are fostering links outside the industry in various ways: pharmaceutical companies in the US are giving increasing financial support to university-based biomedical research. Still others are breaking down large and bureaucratic research establishments into smaller, more agile units.)

THE INNOVATION GAP

These examples typify many sectors of the economy. Corporate performance in the 1980s has been strong: profits and cash flow are up, and productivity is now rising faster than that of our major trading partners. As encouraging as these trends are, however, there remains cause for concern. By far the greatest proportion of the improvement in performance has come from increased efficiency. Excess capacity has been removed. Unprofitable product lines and businesses have been closed. Corporate overheads have been cut. Far less of the improvement has come from adopting truly innovative approaches to new markets and needs. Managers may have recognized the need for innovation. They have yet to translate it into real action.

The quest for improved efficiency is worthwhile, indeed necessary. It must go on as a continuous process. Alone, however, it is insufficient. Unless it is coupled with an innovative approach, the search for efficiency will become sterile, out of touch with customers' needs. This is the challenge facing all of us: filling the innovation gap.

SUMMARY

Managers have recognized the need for innovative approaches to their businesses:

- Response to increased competitive pressures.

- Relevant in all industries.

Real innovative success has, however, lagged behind perceptions of the need to innovate:

- Efficiency has improved, creativity less so.

- Innovative success is actually declining in many industries.

Filling the **Innovation Gap** is a major corporate priority.

2 WHAT IS INNOVATION?

Innovation is not primarily about technology. It is not even about new products or services per se. It is about customers. How can we deliver new or increased value to our customers?

Innovation can take place in any part of the business sytsem – or indeed throughout the whole business system. Unless managers adopt a sufficiently broad definition of innovation they run the risk of missing whole areas of innovative opportunities.

2 WHAT IS INNOVATION?

- The power of definitions

- Successful innovators

- Innovation: a new definition

THE POWER OF DEFINITIONS

The innovation gap is real. The need to become more innovative across a wide spread of activities is perhaps the most pressing challenge which industry faces today. Yet, what exactly do we mean by the term 'innovation'? Which aspects of a firm's operations are included, and which are excluded? We need to define innovation. This is for sound practical reasons, not out of academic interest. Definitions determine perceptions. Perceptions drive action. Defining innovation correctly is therefore the vital first step in making our companies more innovative.

Ask most business people to define innovation and two or three dominant themes tend to emerge:

- **Technology:** many people define innovation to be the development of a new technology, or its application to a specific use. Innovation and R&D lie side by side. Although the innovation must be aimed at providing some product or service for customers, technology is the driving force. Technology is what makes it possible.

- **Products or services:** innovation is normally taken to mean a new product or service. Its effect is experienced directly by customers. The process of innovation culminates in the launch on to the market of the new concept. Other types of innovation – such as in the manufacturing process, the distribution method, or other aspects of the business system – are included only relatively rarely.

- **Randomness:** innovation is usually considered to be inherently random in nature. It relies more than anything upon some creative spark of genius. The critical input is made by one person acting in isolation. Without a creative genius like this, there can be no innovation. The whole process, therefore, is difficult to manage: either you have a genius or you don't.

Every aspect of how managers and companies approach the whole issue of innovation – where they look for it, how they organize for it, how they evaluate it and how they implement it – is determined by these basic perceptions. Figure 4 shows some of the most commonly held views and the management implications which flow from them. These perceptions form an implicit definition of innovation.

Figure 4: Basic perceptions determine how companies approach innovation

Perceptions	Technology	Product/service	Randomness
	• Innovation is driven by new technological developments	• Innovation relates directly to a new product or service	• The process of innovation is inherently random

Innovation is unimportant in industries which are:
• low-tech
• mature

Innovation can be pursued independently from the day-to-day running of the company

Innovation is the responsibility primarily of the R&D department

Innovation relates to new products and services, not to new ways of running existing businesses

Impetus for innovation comes from one department
• others contribute in a secondary supporting role

Implications

They have far-reaching implications in several areas:

- **Mature industries:** if innovation is synonymous with technology, then what role does it have in mature or low-tech industries? Clearly not much. Some industries are considered to be simply more amenable to innovation than others. Attempting to innovate in the latter type of industry is unlikely to be fruitful. Efforts are better invested elsewhere. Managers in mature industries often assume that innovation is simply not important for their company's future success.

- **Technology:** if innovation is closely linked to technology, then the responsibility for it should be given to the R&D department. It can be taken out of the mainstream of the organization and considered as a stand-alone activity.

- **Responsibility for innovation:** since innovation relates to the product or service per se, then it is their design which should drive the process. One department, typically R&D, design or marketing, has the leading role to play, while all others, finance, personnel, manufacturing, distribution etc. are of secondary importance. Their role is essentially supportive rather than creative. They must fit in with the innovative plans of the department which is leading the effort.

- **Management:** the randomness of the innovative process means that it cannot be managed in the same way as other aspects of the firm's operations. There either are or are not creative geniuses within the firm. If there are, then the firm will be innovative. If there are not, then it will not be. The best that can be done is to ensure that they are given the maximum creative freedom, perhaps by setting up an independent department outside the main body of the organization.

- **Integration:** the focus on the product or service itself, together with the fact that innovation is often considered to be the responsibility of a separate specialist department, promotes the view that innovations are not so much new ways of looking at the existing business, but rather that they are stand-alone add-ons. Innovation becomes additive rather than integrative, with limited impact on the firm's base business.

SUCCESSFUL INNOVATORS

How does this view of innovation correspond with reality? In particular, how does the approach which it suggests compare with what successful innovative firms actually do? A few examples of innovators from a range of industries will help to provide some answers:

- *Toyota's Production System (Just-In-Time) has revolutionized how companies worldwide think about manufacturing. In this system the factory operates with zero inventory of part-finished products. To realize this goal, each stage of the production line must receive the parts it needs in exactly the right quantity and at exactly the right time. By achieving this, the system eliminates the need for wasteful storage of work-in-progress and expensive multiple handling of parts into and out of store. It has given Toyota a formidable advantage over its competitors in terms of production cost, quality and the breadth of product range which is possible. The system has been emulated and copied by manufacturing companies worldwide.*

- *Bank One is a large mid-western US bank. It grew extremely rapidly and profitably in the late 1970s and 1980s by focusing on becoming an efficient low cost processor of credit card and other transactions. It provides these services for client banks in every state of the US. Its processing skills lie behind the innovative efforts of many other banks. (For example it provided the transactions processing required for Merrill Lynch's revolutionary cash-management account in 1977.)*

- *Mini mills have altered the face of the steel industry in several countries. In place of the traditional huge integrated steelworks using iron ore as their raw material, the mini mill uses steel scrap. Their minimum economic size is a fraction that of an integrated steel works. Using inexpensive steel scrap and far less energy than an integrated steelworks, they have a fundamentally more attractive cost structure for the production of basic steels. This enables them to be highly competitive in their local markets. Mini mills have prospered even while the integrated steelmakers have faced major losses and chronic overcapacity.*

- *Kwik-Fit built the market in the UK for car tyre and exhaust fitting centres. It has over 350 outlets nationwide which specialize in giving motorists a rapid, high quality and inexpensive fitting service. It has eclipsed the traditional full service repair garages: today over 60 per cent of new exhausts are supplied through fitting centres.*

- *Direct Line is an insurance business set up in 1985 by the Royal Bank of Scotland. It sells policies direct to individual customers, bypassing the traditional distribution channel of the insurance broker. It adopts a highly automated systems approach which enables it to save costs at the same time as delivering superior levels of service. In this highly competitive business it has grown rapidly to present a serious challenge to the established leaders in the industry.*

■ *Federal Express has fundamentally changed the whole nature of the express package industry. By introducing its now famous hub-and-spoke collection and distribution system, it stole a major lead on the established competitors in the industry. The fundamental cost advantages inherent in Federal's approach have enabled it to address completely new segments of the market and establish an unassailable lead.*

Six examples from six different industries. Together they provide some important insights into the true nature of innovation:

- **Technology vs customers:** for none of them was a technological advance the key driving force behind the innovation. They all exploited the technological opportunities that were available to them, but in no case was that the central concept behind the new business idea. In each case it was a strategic vision which created the opportunity. Each one was the direct result of managers adopting a fundamentally new approach to existing problems: they redefined their businesses and found new ways of delivering value to their customers.

- **Product vs business system:** in each case it was innovation throughout the whole business system which created the new value, rather than in the product or service per se. In some examples – such as Toyota's Production System – there is no new product with which one can identify the innovation: its value lies in changing the way in which existing products or services are produced and delivered to customers. In others, such as Direct Line's insurance policies, the innovation did result in the launch of a new product on to the market. Even in these cases, however, it was not the product itself which created the innovation's true distinctiveness – after all, one motor insurance policy is very much like any other one. Rather, it was the way in which the product was produced and delivered to customers – how the whole business system worked – which created the new value.

- **Insight vs implementation:** each innovation was founded upon one brilliantly simple insight - Taichi Ohno of Toyota's realization that cars could be produced more efficiently in small batches and with no wasteful inventory lying around, or Frank Smith of Federal Express's idea that a hub-and-spoke system with one massive central sorting operation was the most efficient way to run an overnight package service. Translating them from concept to reality was a different story, however. Each one required years of effort on the part of managers and workers from all parts of the company – refining the concept, adding to it and modifying it in countless ways. Toyota's Production System took over 30 years to perfect. Employees make over two million suggestions per year for improvements to the process, 96 per cent of which are implemented. Hardly the work of a single specialist department. Successful innovation becomes integrated into the very fabric of the firm. It involves all departments and levels within the company.

- **Mature industries:** several of the examples are from mature, low-tech industries – steel, car exhausts, manufacturing. Innovation is possible in all industries.

- **Isolated event vs ongoing process:** perhaps what distinguishes many of these innovators most is how they have made innovation into an ongoing process, rather than a one-off event. It has become a frame of mind, a basic foundation of the company's whole strategy. Toyota's Production System is a constantly evolving entity, not just a set of rules and procedures. Kwik-Fit and Federal Express are constantly experimenting with developments and variants of their original concept.

INNOVATION: A NEW DEFINITION

A new definition of innovation is needed – one which encompasses all the possible types, together with their organizational and managerial implications. The traditional technology/product focus is clearly inadequate: by concentrating attention upon these two aspects at the expense of others it blinkers and limits management's perspective on innovation. Entire areas are left out of the search. Potentially attractive opportunities are passed by. Innovation becomes relegated to the role of searching for additional products or services, rather than being what it should be: a core part of the firm's overall strategy. By doing this, the traditional approach limits our ability to be truly innovative, to fill the innovation gap.

A more useful definition is:

[New ways of delivering customer value]

There are four central strands to the definition:

- **New:** innovation requires identifying new ways of solving existing problems and meeting the market's requirements, not optimizing the current set-up. There will always be ways to fine-tune the existing situation: careful attention to costs and operations can bring a product's or service's price down over time; continuous attention to market research and customers' comments can ensure its continued relevance as those customers' needs evolve. These are necessary and must continue, but alone they are insufficient. Innovation calls for different ways of satisfying basic needs, not just doing existing tasks better. It requires lateral thinking. Existing moulds and patterns of behaviour have to be broken and cast aside.

  ■ *Kwik-Fit did not 'improve' upon the offering of existing motor repair shops. Instead, it found a completely new way of addressing one very narrow, well defined aspect of car owners' repair needs. Its narrow focus on exhausts and tyres enabled it to reap significant purchasing and operating economies. It passes these on to its customers in the form of rapid, high quality service and keen prices.*

  ■ *Integrated steelworks had been around for decades when the first mini-mills appeared. The integrated plants had undergone continuous improvement and were close to the limits of their potential performance. All this was insufficient to protect them from the onslaught of the mini mills: their fundamental economic advantages (in terms of raw materials and energy) were simply too powerful. They represented a different (and dramatically superior) way of making basic steels. Optimization is necessary – but it cannot hold back innovation.*

- **Delivery:** innovation need not relate only to the product or service itself – it can apply to any part of the business system or value chain* associated with delivering a product or service to a customer. Toyota innovated in the manufacturing part of its value chain, with major beneficial effects for cost, product quality and model range. Federal Express innovated by competing on the basis of a completely new and

---

* *The value chain, developed by Michael Porter (in* Competitive Advantage, *Free Press, 1985), is a diagrammatic representation of a firm's operations. It shows the major activities in each of several different areas, and the links which operate between them. (See Chapter 4,* Looking for Innovation, *for further detail.)*

different value chain: it replaced the point-to-point approach of its competitors with a hub-and-spoke system. Innovation, therefore, can consist of changes to a particular link in the value chain, or to the creation of a fundamentally new value chain, bypassing the traditional approach. The grocery retail business provides many good examples:

■ *Figure 5 shows a schematic value chain for the business, together with some of the areas in which innovations have taken place. The leading companies in the industry have innovated in one or more individual links of the chain (e.g. changes to the retail environment itself, the introduction of central warehousing, or the development of own-brand groceries).*

Figure 5: Grocery retailers have innovated in all parts of the value chain

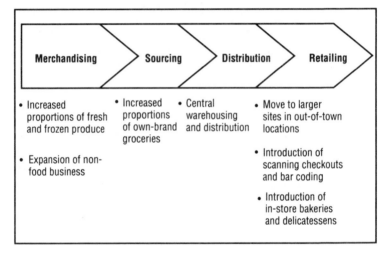

■ *Others have created entirely new value chains. A new breed of bulk grocery retailers has identified an opportunity to provide a narrow range of products (basic dry groceries) in a new format (loose, unbranded) through specific types of outlets (small, low cost stores which have been passed over by other grocery retailers as they have increasingly moved to larger sites out of town). The whole sector has been growing extremely rapidly, with several new entrants competing to exploit this newly identified market niche.*

● **Customer:** all too often the search for innovation is internally driven – how can we perform this function better? How can we optimize this process? Unless it is related directly to customers' needs, however, such internal optimization is worth little. Truly successful innovation is always driven by a careful consideration of customers' needs rather than internal constraints. In many cases the innovation may even result in lower levels of efficiency, as measured by narrow internal measures. That need not matter, however, if the innovation meets customers' real needs in a better way than the previously available solution:

■ *Manufacturers of wall fixings compete very stongly on price, with relatively undifferentiated products. Hilti, however, recognized that builders do not want to buy a fixing as such, rather they want to buy the ability to fix an item to a wall. This observation led the company to develop a new system of fixings and tools which, although individually expensive as components, lead to overall economies through higher labour productivity. By concentrating on the customer's economics – rather than its own – Hilti was able to innovate.*

■ *Industrial hoses come in a wide range of sizes and types of material. For many years manufacturers and national chains of distributors have competed strongly on price for standard products for the high volume applications. A small distributor in Southampton, however, has established a profitable niche in large diameter hoses for marine diesel applications. It offers its customers a 24-hour, 365-day-a-year service. In situations where a large ship might be stuck in port for the want of three feet of hose, the firm can charge high prices and still offer good value: its customers are buying a mobile ship, not a piece of hose.*

■ *A Belgian biotechnology company has just developed a sugar beet plant which is resistant to most common weedkillers. If successful, this will enable farmers to use one application of an inexpensive weedkiller rather than a combination of several specific and expensive herbicides as they do at present. Sugar beet farmers spend two to three times as much money on weed control as they do on seeds. The potential cost savings to them are therefore significant – even though the seeds themselves will be more expensive.*

● **Value:** the search for innovation must be motivated by the will to offer the customer that which he values more than his current product or service. Sometimes this means a higher performance product. Sometimes, however, it means a lower performance – with greater simplicity/convenience/availability/affordability etc. What it always means, however, is identifying unsatisfied needs – either among customers as a whole, or more frequently in some segment. There are often many different ways of creating new customer value within one industry.

■ *As consumer wealth has increased, so motorcycles have in large part moved from being a mode of transport into being a form of recreation. In addition to this, most users who do need their motorbikes for transport now also demand high performance, sophistication and sporty looks. Manufacturers have responded to this trend by developing ever more refined, powerful – and expensive – products. They have done this very well. A Midlands motorcycle dealer reasoned, however, that there were also customers who did want a basic, no frills, cheap machine. They signed up the UK distributorship for MZ, and started importing inexpensive East European motorcycles which sell at below 50 per cent of the price of an equivalent size Japanese model. They now have a market share of 24 per cent of the commuter bike sector of the market. This technically inferior but inexpensive product clearly represents 'value' for one segment of customers.*

■ *In the same industry, Norton Villiers Triumph identified a need among its target customers – successful, mature people who had previously been motorcyclists – for a high quality, high price British motorcycle. Having owned a motorcycle in earlier years, they would now like one for recreational use, but are not attracted to the German or Japanese machines available (partly a desire to buy British, partly a wish for a motorbike which must have excellent handling and build quality, rather than the ultimate in out-and-out performance which these models offer). It launched the rotary-engined Commander and Classic models into the police and consumer markets. Both are selling well. Most importantly, it is attracting back motorcycling enthusiasts who might never have bought another machine; it has created a new segment.*

Innovation is a very broad subject. It encompasses every aspect of a firm, how it operates and its relationships with its customers. Many of the most significant innovations have little or nothing to do with new technology. Many of them occur in mature, low-tech industries. They all have one thing in common, however. They represent new ways of delivering value to customers. Innovation, therefore, is central to the much broader issue of how it is that firms deliver value to their customers.

It is important to adopt a correspondingly broad definition of innovation. Only by doing so can management ensure that they exploit fully all the opportunities for delivering new customer value which exist in every industry. Only by doing so can they fill the innovation gap.

SUMMARY

Innovation is not primarily concerned with technology. It is not even about new products or services per se

. . . it is about **new ways of delivering customer value.**

it is important to adopt this **broad definition** of innovation

. . . otherwise companies will not explore the full range of opportunities open to them.

- Potentially major areas will be missed.

3 STRATEGIC AND TACTICAL INNOVATION

True innovation is fundamentally strategic in nature. Its objective is to create defensible competitive advantage for the firm. Unless it does this it is merely tactical, not strategic. It may give some short-term increase in sales and margin, but is unlikely to result in long-term strategic success. The search for innovation must be integrated into the company's overall strategy development. It is therefore a primary responsibility of top management.

3 STRATEGIC AND TACTICAL INNOVATION

- Competitive advantage

- Changing the equilibrium

- Discontinuities and innovation

- Strategic innovation

- Business system innovation

COMPETITIVE ADVANTAGE

The key determinant of any business's long-term success is its ability to build and defend a competitive advantage. The competitive advantage can consist of either a lower cost position than the firm's competitors or the ability to achieve higher prices as a result of some perceived uniqueness in the market. Michael Porter identifies* three generic strategies for achieving such an advantage: differentiation, overall cost leadership and focus.

The link between competitive advantage and success is borne out time after time by experience. Firms without a tangible competitive advantage seldom prosper for very long. They may do well while the market is growing or when competition is not intense. They are extremely unlikely to perform in the long term, however. Sooner or later the market's growth slows, and competitive pressures mount. When this happens such firms' performance deteriorates rapidly. This link between profitability and competitive advantage is the very cornerstone of strategy. In fact, one useful working definition of strategy is that it is the process of achieving and maintaining competitive advantage in a business.

In the late 1960s through to the late 1970s, strategic planning reigned supreme. The results, however, were often disappointing. An excessive focus on strategy formulation at the expense of effective implementation

---

*Michael E. Porter Competitive Strategy (Free Press, 1980).

had the predictable mediocre results. The late 1970s and early 1980s brought a natural backlash. It had become fashionable to discard strategy in favour of 'tight operations', 'sticking to the knitting', a 'commitment to excellence', and so on. Truly successful businessmen and women have always adhered to these principles in one sense or another, however. They recognize the current vogue in business thinking for what it is: a swing of the pendulum. In place of the earlier (excessive) focus on planning and strategy, we now have an (excessive) focus on day-to-day operational aspects of management. All our truly excellent companies – large and small – achieve a healthy balance between the two. Good strategy and good operations are both necessary for superior performance. Neither is sufficient alone. Focus on one to the exclusion of the other guarantees mediocre performance.

The nature of strategy itself has evolved in the intervening period, however. Fifteen years ago the business world was fairly simple compared to today. Success in most industries was inextricably linked to market share. Companies competed for dominance in their industry, with relatively less attention given to segment-focused or specialized strategies. Higher market share usually meant lower costs, improved market power and, with them, the ability to squeeze competitors yet further.

Since then a number of factors have changed:

- Slower economic growth and excess capacity have fundamentally altered the economics of many industries. Investing to pre-emptively gain market share is no longer a viable strategy. Efficient utilization of existing capacity and accurately targeting customer needs are much more important.

  - *Taichi Ohno described Toyota's approach to car manufacturing: 'It's a wrong notion to believe that mass production will guarantee you less cost. That was true in the 1960s, in those days, where there was a high demand. But that notion has become a myth that no longer applies in the 1980s. Now production capacity exceeds demand. For some reason many people in the world still believe in this myth and they still take for granted that if they increase mass production they can reduce costs.'*

- Many industries have reached the limits of economies to scale: today increased market share need not imply lower costs, but often the reverse. Higher volumes sometimes bring only increased complexity and higher overheads.

  - *In the 1960s and 1970s the brewing industry invested in ever larger breweries, which offered significant economies in production cost.*

Recently, however, a small number of pubs has been established, each with its own integrated miniature brewery. Although the brewing cost itself is higher, the saving on transport is such that the total delivered cost is very similar to having beer delivered from a major brewery.

- Technological and other changes have created new opportunities in many industries for smaller competitors. Their costs need no longer be so disadvantaged relative to the market leaders. On the contrary, by exploiting the latest techniques (e.g. flexible manufacturing systems) and focusing on particular segments they can sometimes enjoy distinct cost advantages relative to more established competitors (see Chapter 8, Less can be More).

- Customers' requirements are becoming ever more sophisticated and, through this, segmented. One approach, one solution is no longer adequate in most industries. There is room for numerous competitors to succeed, each satisfying the needs of a specific type of customer.

One result of these changes is that most industries now afford many more potential ways of gaining a competitive advantage. Some customers might want low price, while others need great reliability. Some need excellent delivery or service above all, while yet others need a particular technical specification. And so on. Seldom can one supplier satisfy all needs. There is a natural role for several different approaches to what may superficially appear to be one market. Rather than pursuing a monolithic strategy to obtain market share, success now calls for identifying inadequately satisfied needs, and developing new ways of delivering value to those customers.

CHANGING THE EQUILIBRIUM

These changes to the business environment have made the task of strategy development more challenging – but also far more rewarding. With so many more opportunities to create a competitive advantage, the payoff to creative, innovative strategies can be tremendous. Most industries continue in a state of competitive equilibrium until disturbed by some force. In that equilibrium the relative positions and strengths of the various competitors remain broadly constant. The essence of strategy is to **change the competitive equilibrium** to a new point of equilibrium more favourable to oneself. It is only by achieving this new, more favourable equilibrium that true value can be created for the firm.

There are two basic ways in which the competitive equilibrium in an industry can be changed:

- By a process of continuous, or natural, competition. In it competitors operate in a broadly constant way, but seek to make incremental changes to their positions. In effect, they are competing within a constant market framework, within the confines of a single conceptual map (see Chapter 13, Innovation and Conceptual Maps).

- By the appearance of **discontinuities**, where some fundamental change takes place in the way in which the industry operates. By their very nature, these discontinuities upset the existing equilibrium, and provide alert competitors with opportunities to achieve step-change improvements to their competitive positions. Examples of such discontinuities abound:

  - *major technological changes*
  - *changes in legislation or regulation*
  - *the emergence of new, low cost competitors*
  - *innovation.*

DISCONTINUITIES AND INNOVATION

The continuous/discontinuous distinction is an important one to draw, with major implications for firms' efforts to improve their competitive positions. By their very nature, continuous changes are gradual: market share and position change only slowly under the forces of natural competition. More than this, unless one is lucky enough to have incompetent competitors, market share gains are likely to be fiercely contested. With a slowly changing situation, competitors have time to respond to any losses they have incurred. The result is often a protracted and costly battle for market share. When discontinuities occur, however, the whole competitive situation is different. Firms which exploit the discontinuity successfully can often make major step-change improvements in their competitive position before their adversaries realize what is going on, far less are able to respond to it. Instead of a grim and drawn-out battle in the trenches, a whole new competitive front can be opened up – one in which the aggressor has the initiative and can determine the new rules of competition. Discontinuities provide unique opportunities to improve competitive position and create value for the firm. Discontinuities and innovation are inextricably linked:

- Every discontinuity changes the ground rules of competition in some way. It creates a new framework within which the players in the industry must compete. It therefore creates innovative opportunities.

- Among all types of discontinuity, innovation is the only one which is directly under management's control. It represents their greatest opportunity to create favourable discontinuities and, through this, to improve their competitive position.

Profitability, strategy, discontinuities and innovation are interwoven (see Figure 6). Superior profitability requires having a sound strategy. Exploiting discontinuities is one of the central features of successful strategy development. Discontinuities in turn give rise to innovative opportunities. Innovation is therefore one of the key strategic responsibilities of senior management.

Figure 6:   Profitability, strategy, discontinuities and innovation are inextricably interwoven. Innovation is a key responsibility of senior management.

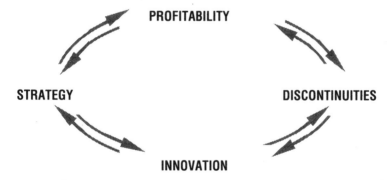

PROFITABILITY

STRATEGY

DISCONTINUITIES

INNOVATION

STRATEGIC INNOVATION

Considering innovation in a strategic rather than a tactical context adds a new perspective. Truly successful innovation does not just lead to some extra sales volume, or a temporary improvement in performance. At heart, it is not even a question of new products or services. Rather, it is about achieving a fundamental improvement in competitive position, about re-establishing the competitive equilibrium at a new, more favourable point. To do this it must not only create value for customers, but must do so in a way which gives the innovator a **defensible competitive advantage** (see Figure 7). Without this the innovation is tactical, not strategic. It may provide some additional sales and profit, but is unlikely to result in long-term strategic success.

Figure 7: Strategically successful innovation requires establishing a defensible competitive advantage.

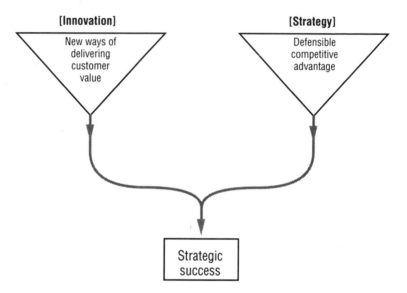

The history of innovation is fraught with examples of individuals and firms which, although they innovated well, did not establish a defensible competitive advantage at the same time. Strategically, they failed. In business terms, they failed. They did not reap the benefits of their innovation:

- *Osborne Computer invented the portable personal computer and played a major role in developing the market. It failed to establish a defensible position, however, and lost ground to a host of imitators. It subsequently filed for bankruptcy under Chapter 11 on 13 September 1983.*

- *Laker Airways identified the latent demand for cheap transatlantic travel. With a fleet of three used DC10s it prospered for a while. The entrenched competitors responded fiercely once Laker reached a size where it was damaging their revenues. By introducing aggressive and increasingly sophisticated pricing schedules they hit Laker extremely hard. With its fleet of only three aircraft and no secure volume from feeder airlines, Laker found it difficult to respond: it had no secure competitive advantage. The firm eventually left the business.*

To the search for new ways of delivering customer value must be added a search for defensible competitive advantage. If an innovation offers the firm no prospect of establishing a tangible competitive advantage - or if any advantage is likely to be transient – then the innovation is unlikely to be a business success. Either alternative ways of building competitive advantage must be found, or the innovation should not be pursued.

At what point in the innovation process should consideration of the strategic factors begin? At the very earliest point possible. There are often a number of different ways in which to pursue and structure an innovative opportunity. The firm can proceed alone or form alliances with other companies. It can focus on specific groups of customers or upon the market as a whole. There may be a range of sourcing and distribution options open to it. The particular way chosen normally has major implications for the extent of the competitive advantage which can be realized. If strategic implications are only considered later on in the process, then there is a very real risk that fundamental and irrevocable decisions will have been made. These may severely limit the opportunities for competitive advantage and profit. It is all too easy to press ahead down one particular avenue in the rush to make the innovation a reality. If this precludes an analysis of all the strategic options there is a real risk that the firm can become locked into a suboptimal – or even unviable – position. Innovators ignore strategic analysis at their peril.

BUSINESS SYSTEM INNOVATION

A great deal has already been written about competitive advantage and, in particular, the various potential sources of advantage which can be exploited: economies of scale or focus, experience, superior price realization and so on. All of these are relevant to innovation and should be explored. One type of competitive advantage is of particular importance in innovation: that which derives from **integration of advantage throughout the value chain**. In other words, rather than having a competitive advantage in just one or two parts of the value chain, these innovators enjoy competitive advantages in all or several parts of it. They achieve this by **innovating** in the **business system** itself.

The essence of their innovation is not so much the nature of the customer value itself, but rather the way in which that value is delivered. Some of the most spectacularly successful innovations have been of this type:

■ *Toyota's Production System (Just In Time) is a major source of advantage for the company. Despite similar wage levels, the average Japanese car costs only two-thirds as much to produce as the average American car. The system is founded upon some simple but fundamental beliefs about how cars should be produced. In practice, however, it is much more than a production system. It impinges upon every single aspect of the firm's operations: from personnel policy to relationships with suppliers, from production scheduling to delivery of finished products. Perhaps its most fundamental influence is on the company's product range: its flexibility makes a wide choice feasible at a realistic cost.*

■ *Benetton's business system is shown schematically in Figure 8. It has innovated in almost every aspect of its operations, giving it significant advantages. Four areas are worth special mention:*

   ★ *Its distinctive designs and use of colour give it a strong consumer brand and a clear theme throughout its international marketing programme.*

   ★ *Its overall design philosophy and manufacturing set-up have enabled it to adopt piece dyeing techniques. (Whole garments or individual components such as sleeves are made up in neutral colours to be dyed at a later stage.) This cuts down lead times in the factory and increases manufacturing flexibility. Benetton can respond extremely rapidly to changes in market conditions and demands. The benefits are threefold: the firm's working capital investment in stock is reduced, returns are minimized, and it can keep its shops stocked with the fastest selling items.*

   ★ *Every shop is linked through a computer network to the factory. Detailed information on how well individual lines and colours are selling is fed back to the centre on a daily basis. Detailed revisions to the production schedule can be implemented extremely rapidly.*

   ★ *Benetton controls its retail outlets. This gives it far greater control over the merchandising and selling of its products, an advantage which few clothing manufacturers enjoy. With a large international network of stores, it can experiment with changes to layout and product mix at limited risk before introducing widespread changes.*

Figure 8: Benetton demonstrates innovation throughout the whole business system.

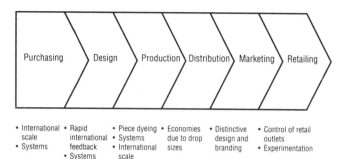

Purchasing	Design	Production	Distribution	Marketing	Retailing
• International scale • Systems	• Rapid international feedback • Systems	• Piece dyeing • Systems • International scale	• Economies due to drop sizes	• Distinctive design and branding	• Control of retail outlets • Experimentation

There are numerous other examples of firms that have innovated throughout their overall business system: MFI in furniture retail; Kwik-Fit in exhausts; Direct Line in insurance; Federal Express in courier services, and so on. Business system integration is of particular importance for sound strategic reasons.

- Innovation is needed in several different areas. Not only must each area be right, but there must also be congruence between them. The whole concept has to fit together. Competitors therefore find it harder to copy. Several aspects of the innovation typically relate to internal operations. These are generally more difficult to comprehend and copy than, say, a new product design. Business system innovation therefore often leads to more **defensible competitive advantage** than other, narrower types of innovation.

- For exactly the same reasons, however, business system innovation is very difficult to achieve. With innovation taking place in several areas, there is simply more to go wrong. It is therefore often the most demanding type of innovation for a firm to embark upon – but it can also be the most rewarding.

Far too many businessmen think of innovation as being only about new products or services. It is not. It is fundamentally strategic in nature. It is about delivering new customer value and changing the rules of competition. It is about creating defensible competitive advantage. Innovation therefore has an increasingly important strategic role to play. It is of central concern to top management.

SUMMARY

Innovation is inextricably linked to **profitability**, **competitive advantage** and **discontinuities**.

- Superior profitability requires establishing a competitive advantage.
- Exploiting discontinuities provides the best way to increase the firm's competitive advantage.
- Innovation is the greatest source of favourable discontinuities.

. . . innovation must be a priority for top management.

Business system innovation is a particularly important source of defensible competitive advantage.

- Often difficult for competitors to copy.

II THE INNOVATIVE PROCESS

4 LOOKING FOR INNOVATION

The search for innovation relies on insight, creativity, luck . . . and hard work. None of these are random. They can be managed. Management can be effective at two levels. Firstly, they can ensure that the company's environment encourages and supports innovation. Secondly, they can take specific actions to generate innovative opportunities. Done properly, these two levels reinforce each other.

Few firms manage their innovative efforts sufficiently actively. They are missing opportunities. They are weakening their own long-term competitive position.

4 LOOKING FOR INNOVATION

- A flow of ideas

- Managing the flow at two levels

- Specific actions
  - Macro trends
  - Translation
  - Analogy
  - Unexplained successes and failures
  - Technological limits and enabling changes
  - Discontinuities
  - Value chains

- Closing the loop

A FLOW OF IDEAS

Innovating requires that managers must generate a flow of new ideas for evaluation. Experience shows that a high proportion of all innovative ventures will fail. There should therefore always be many more ideas generated than are actually used. Without a steady stream of new concepts, there are significant risks: in their desire to innovate, managers can rush into new ventures without sufficient care or discrimination. If the firm is not rejecting several proposals for every one which it pursues, there is something wrong. It will almost certainly be investing in new ventures which a more careful analysis would have shown to be flawed. How can managers generate the flow of new ideas they need? Where can they look for innovation? Can the search be made more systematic, or would such a move be counter-productive? Would attempting to manage the process merely stifle the creativity which is driving it in the first place? Beyond the overall level of innovative activity, can management usefully direct the search in particular directions?

Brilliant insights clearly have an important role to play – many major advances have indeed resulted from one person's vision, pursued against all the odds. Sony's Walkman, 3M's Post-It adhesive notepads and Smith Kline & French's Tagamet anti-ulcer drug were all pushed forward by lone product champions for a long time before they finally broke through. (What is highly relevant, of course, is that they did this within organizations which tolerated and supported such behaviour. The culture in some companies positively encourages managers to pursue their own ideas if they have the conviction to do so. In other companies, this simply does not happen). Nayak and Ketteringham in their book *Breakthroughs** go so far as to say that important innovations are inherently random in nature: they result from the work of individuals pursuing an idea with missionary zeal, often for personal rather than business reasons. They identify the primary driving force as the individual's desire to prove his or her new concept, to make it happen. While there may be some truth in this view, it ignores some absolutely central issues. By implication, this view of innovation as an essentially random process suggests that there is little that management can do actively to promote and search for innovation within their companies. Nothing could be further from the truth: the innovation process can and should be managed. It must be managed.

MANAGING THE FLOW AT TWO LEVELS

Innovation will never be deterministic: there will always be a high degree of uncertainty involved in searching for and developing new opportunities. What management can do is to influence the search for innovation within their companies to improve their chances of success. They can act at two different levels to increase the flow of new ideas:

- **Environmental:** creating an environment within the firm – culturally, organizationally and strategically – which supports and encourages innovative activity.

- **Specific:** taking specific actions to generate individual ideas for evaluation.

Getting the environment right is extremely difficult. It encompasses a wide diversity of factors: the firm's culture and belief system, its

---

* *P. R. Nayak and J. M. Ketteringham*, Breakthroughs (*Rawson Associates, 1986*).

organization structure and reporting relationships, personnel measurement and motivation, career structures and the way in which innovation itself is monitored within the firm. These are all fairly soft issues. There are no universally right answers and few wrong ones. Within some extremely broad guidelines, the most appropriate solution depends upon the individual firm and its particular situation. Most importantly, complex tradeoffs must be made before opting for a particular approach, for example:

- How should the firm be organized? On the one hand, small cross-functional teams may be very effective in creative terms (see Chapter 9, Organizing for Innovation), while on the other hand, narrow functional specialization may be more efficient for the firm's day-to-day operations. Which structure makes most sense in overall terms?

- How can the firm's culture be managed? A probing, questioning culture is a pre-requisite for successful strategic innovation. The existing conceptual map has to be challenged. Conversely, commitment to a single shared vision can unite and focus the firm's efforts. Where does the best compromise lie?

In addition, many of these environmental factors are difficult to change. A new culture cannot be introduced overnight by dictat. Meaningful advances take a lot of time and tremendous patience to introduce. Managers have two types of tool at their disposal to effect the changes they desire. Firstly, they can take direct action on the environment itself by, for instance, influencing the firm's culture through their own words and actions, or adjusting standard personnel measurements and career structures to accommodate innovation better. Is the innovative performance of the firm measured in any way? Are successful innovators rewarded? What are the penalties for failure?* Equally important, however, is the effect which taking specific actions – i.e. pursuing individual opportunities – has on the overall environment. It reinforces the changes which are taking place already. The two types of action – environmental and specific – feed off each other (see Figure 9).

- Each small positive change to the environment makes generating the next new idea that much easier.

---

* These aspects are discussed in further detail in other chapters: Chapter 10, Innovation and the Mature Company; Chapter 12, Innovations and Innovativeness; and Chapter 14, Adaptive and Repetitive Behaviour.

- Each individual idea generated and pursued is an opportunity to reinforce the cultural and organizational changes which are taking place.

Figure 9: Environmental and specific actions reinforce each other in improving the firm's innovative performance.

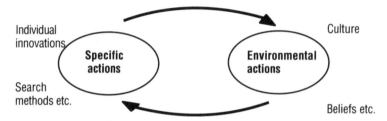

SPECIFIC ACTIONS

The purpose of this chapter is to consider some of the specific actions which managers can take to help generate innovative ideas. Of course it requires luck – but to a large extent we create our own good fortune through diligence and perseverance. Innovation is about creating new value by identifying different ways of approaching existing problems. This requires creativity and inspiration – but above all it needs a frame of mind that is tuned in to the right frequency. What adopting these specific approaches can do is to force management's thinking and energies on to these frequencies and ensure that no avenues are left unexplored. Often they will help to generate new ideas directly. In other cases it is their environmental impact which is the most important. They can help to prepare the ground so that when the germ of a new idea does appear, it is far more likely to be recognized in all its significance and pursued for all it is worth.

There are several approaches which can be used to help generate innovative ideas. Some of them overlap. There is no harm in that: in many cases approaching the same idea from different perspectives can in itself produce valuable insights. The most frequently fruitful approaches are:

- Analysis of **macro trends**

- **Translation** of ideas from one market to another

- **Analogy** with other industries

- Analysis of unexplained **successes**

- Analysis of unexplained **failures**
- **Consideration of technological limits** and **enabling changes**
- Discontinuities
- Analysis of the customer's value chain.

Each one of these can be taken by itself to provide valuable insights and innovative opportunities. Together they constitute a formidable arsenal. Using them can help to tune managers' minds into the right creative frequencies. They can provide the key to unlock the creative energies of the organization.

Macro trends

These can relate either to demographic changes or to other fundamental shifts in the business environment. They may appear to be gradual and hardly worthy of note. Over a period of even a few years, however, they can result in such significant changes to the environment that truly important innovative opportunities are created:

■ *Frank Smith's original idea for Federal Express was developed while he was still at college. He reasoned that developments in the electronic and other industries meant there was an increasing need for high value small packages to be carried around the country as priority items. This was particularly true for spare parts and other emergency consignments. He considered that the existing express package services were not up to the task. Something better was needed. He developed the idea of the now familiar hub-and-spoke system, where packages would be collected locally by truck, flown to one massive and highly automated central sorting operation in Memphis and then flown on to their ultimate delivery for final delivery to the customer, again by truck. The scale of the central operation and high utilization of the aircraft would lead to massive economies once the volume built up sufficiently. Seven years later Federal Express started operating – as the biggest start-up in American business history.*

(Two asides: firstly none of the established competitors copied or independently arrived at the same idea in the intervening period – a testimony to the advantage which innovators often enjoy. Smith's new concept simply ran counter to the perceived wisdom of how things should be done in the industry. It did not fit their conceptual map. Accordingly, they ignored it. Secondly, the majority of Federal's packages are now

letters and general items, rather than electronic components: the broad concept was right, even if the details were revised significantly at a later point. If the basic concept is right, it can always somehow be translated into a real opportunity.)

■ *Grocery retailers in the UK have been moving inexorably towards hypermarkets and large supermarkets in edge-of-town and out-of-town locations. The size of these outlets offers significant operating economies and the valuable consumer benefits of wide product choice and convenient parking for the weekly shopping trip. This trend has been going on for several years. Two significant things have happened as a result:*

★ *Competition for the scarce suitable sites has been intense, particularly in the crowded south-east of England. Land values have soared. In addition, the increasing building quality demanded by the consumer has pushed construction costs through the roof. In 1981 new superstores cost an average of £150 per square foot to build and equip. By 1986 the corresponding figure had reached £600. The strain was beginning to show on the multiple retailers' balance sheets, as they raised debt and equity capital to finance their continued expansion. Superstore retailers require healthy margins to justify their investment in new sites. They cannot easily afford price wars. This has created something of a price umbrella.*

★ *Smaller supermarkets in town had been ignored in the rush to ever larger sites. Many of them became run-down. This created a situation in which the run-down stores performed increasingly poorly, making the growing hypermarket sector look even more attractive by comparison.*

John Fletcher of Barker and Dobson spotted the opportunity which this presented. Small supermarkets were available cheaply. By improving and repositioning them he could create a new source of customer value: the high quality local convenience supermarket. Consumers would use them for secondary shopping trips in between their main weekly ones, in particular for fresh produce. He acquired the ailing Budgen's chain of stores and rapidly turned its performance around.

These and other examples show how fruitful a creative analysis of macro trends can be. It is all too easy to assume that one's competitors will have spotted the same trends and come to the same conclusions. In some cases that may be true. Surprisingly often, however, it is not. These macro trends can represent major innovative opportunities. What is needed is a creative and probing approach to analysing them.

A checklist is extremely valuable. Managers should identify all the key areas which influence their business: technology, customer needs, suppliers, distribution channels, demographic trends, changes in the structure or competitive situation in the customer's industry, competing products etc. They should ask themselves a few basic questions: what has changed in the last five years? The last year? What will change over the next year? The next five years? What are the implications for us? These questions should be incorporated into the annual planning cycle. They should all be considered before managers sign off on them. Conscientiously working through a comprehensive checklist can minimize the risk of missing potentially important trends.

Translation

Translating ideas from one geographic market to another shouldn't really work. We all know our economic theory: perfect markets and competitive forces will ensure that good business ideas will be picked up rapidly in one market and introduced to others. There simply shouldn't be a lot of unexploited opportunities lying around. Yet there are! It is quite amazing how often innovative ideas succeed in one country yet take several years to be introduced elsewhere. All the while the opportunity was there, obvious to anyone who cared to travel to see it. Consumers' tastes appear to be converging in several markets, helped by the increasing internationalization of the media. The scope for translating ideas from one market to others is therefore greater than ever. Many ideas migrate from West to East, starting in California before spreading to the East Coast of the US and Europe. Others start in Europe and spread west to the US, while still others emerge in the Far East before being exported to Europe and the US. Whichever way the flow works, however, it is amazing to see how many innovative ideas can be picked up in this way:

- *Specialized car muffler shops had been in operation in the US for many years when Tom Farmer first saw them in 1970. Doubtless several British motor trade executives had also seen them. They failed to realize their significance, however. Most of them saw car sales as their principal concern, with maintenance as little more than a troublesome sideline. The idea of specialized service outlets did not fit their conceptual maps: it would not work in the UK. Tom recognized it as a major opportunity to change the way in which we maintain and service our cars. He brought the idea back across the Atlantic and opened one service centre. It was followed by a further two within six months. Today Kwik-Fit has over 350 outlets in the UK and 98 in Europe. Not only does it dominate the UK market but it is in a leading position in the expansion of this service concept to mainland Europe.*

■ *Multi-screen cinemas (i.e. those with more than three screens) have prospered in the US for many years. They offer the filmgoer unprecedented choice, and change the whole nature of a night out at the movies. With several films to choose from, the need to plan in advance becomes barely necessary. Beyond the obvious consumer benefits, they bring significant operating economies in several important parts of the theatre's cost structure. It is only relatively recently that they have been introduced to Britain.*

■ *Federal Express changed the face of the American small package delivery business. In some senses, it could even be said to have created the business. It took several years for the hub-and-spoke idea to be introduced seriously into European countries. It is now working on a national basis here, using trucks instead of aircraft. And who's one of the leading players? Federal Express.*

■ *British advertising agencies have developed a new way of competing in their industry, by building integrated marketing and communications services companies. They deliver advertising, public relations, direct marketing, sales promotion, sponsorship, product and retail design and management consulting services. Integrating inputs across several parts of the marketing budget has created added value for their clients. It is now possible to take an overall view of the whole marketing task, rather than to have individual agencies from each specialized discipline fighting for their own share of the total. After the idea had been tried successfully in the UK, the leading firms here – Saatchi and Saatchi, WCRS and WPP – have exported it to the US, where they are now among the leading players in the industry.*

■ *Tie Rack changed the face of tie retailing in the UK. They took ties from being items bought in tailors' shops and department stores along with a shirt or suit into impulse-purchased fashion accessories. They changed the economics by purchasing a large proportion of their needs direct from the manufacturers in the Far East, and selling them through dedicated outlets in high traffic areas. It proved dramatically successful, culminating in a public share subscription in 1987, which was 85-fold oversubscribed, valuing the firm at £50 million. Millions of tourists to London took Tie Rack ties home with them. None of them took the business idea. Tie Rack itself has now taken this simple idea to several overseas markets, with a growing number of outlets in the US, Canada and France.*

■ *Several publishing concepts have been successfully translated from one market to another. Money magazine did very well in the US, with a clear focus on personal finance advice for wealthy individuals. The basic concept was adapted for British readers' interests and launched here successfully as* Family Wealth. *(This provides an interesting example of the frequent need to adapt the original idea for other markets: the word 'family' was added to make it a little less self-centred, and to introduce a note of caring, more in tune with perceived British sensitivities.) More recently, several successful European women's magazines have been introduced with great success into additional markets. A previously moribund sector has been transformed by introducing new ideas from other markets.*

There is a truly astounding number of examples of successful innovations which do well in one market for years before some entrepreneur – often the original innovator - takes them international. In the interim period, the innovations were there for all to see. Countless businessmen must have walked right past them. Even today these opportunities exist. You only have to look for them.

One important caveat. Just because an idea has done well in one market does not guarantee its success in another. Any number of factors might be different, reducing its validity in other markets: different patterns of consumer spending, channels of distribution, relative cost structures or regulatory environments. Blindly taking successful ideas into new markets can fail miserably:

■ *Selling holidays by mail order was extremely successful in Scandinavia. A Swedish company tried the idea in the UK with only limited success. The industry's supply structure and consumers' habits were simply not the same.*

■ *Century 21 achieved great success in the US as a franchised chain of real estate agents. A number of companies have tried to introduce this concept to the UK without success. The UK market is dramatically different to the US: with a far higher proportion of all house moves being within one local area, the value of a national network is less than it is in the US. Additionally, British estate agents are less comfortable with the whole concept of franchising than their American counterparts. (The financial services revolution in the UK may now be changing all of this. With the need to provide a far wider range of services than before, the importance of being part of a large network – for systems, training, advertising, etc. – is increasing.)*

Once a potentially worthwhile opportunity has been spotted in some other market, the real work can begin. The concept should be distilled down to its basics:

* ★ *What is the new value that it delivers to customers?*
* ★ *How does it do this? How do the economics stack up?*
* ★ *What products or services does it compete against? What are their cost structures?*
* ★ *What suppliers does it rely upon for critical inputs?*
* ★ *What are the key features of the customers and their industry structure (if appropriate)?*
* ★ *Upon what key hypotheses and assumptions does the concept rest?*

This understanding enables managers to address the question of transferability: will it work in our market? The clearer an understanding they have of the concept, the better they will be able to make this judgement. Significant differences will always exist between different markets. This need not imply that the idea cannot be transferred, rather that it must be adapted. The real skill lies in spotting which differences can be accommodated, and which are so fundamental as to invalidate the idea.

Translation of successful ideas into new markets is no guarantee of success. It does not remove the need for detailed, thorough strategic analysis. What it can do is to provide a stream of ideas for evaluation. Many of them will not turn out to be appropriate for other markets. Some will be spectacular successes.

Analogy

Borrowing ideas from other industries can provide powerful insights into one's own business. Every industry, indeed every segment, is unique. Often, however, the way in which things are done in one industry can give ideas for new approaches in others. Often there will be very good reasons why the approach that works so well in one business is not appropriate elsewhere. Sometimes, however, it just hasn't been thought of yet, and there are real opportunites to transform the business by introducing new ideas. Examples abound:

■ *Eddy Shah had been a television production manager before joining the* Manchester Evening News. *When he started to set up his own business he looked closely at 'free sheets', freely distributed newssheets which carried advertising and minimal or no editorial content. He compared this to the television industry, where advertising revenue paid for lavish programme production. He put the two ideas together and came up with the first free regional* **newspapers** *with a good mix of editorial and advertising content. Free newspapers have since become the outstanding success story of the whole industry. (There is an interesting twist here. Shah knew relatively little about newspaper production, never having seen a letterpress machine in action. He didn't know what wasn't possible, so he went straight to offset presses and direct entry of text by the journalists. The result was a major cost advantage for Messenger Group over its rivals, in addition to the advantage which its novel marketing position had created. Outsiders often enjoy similar advantages: they can take a fresh look at the whole business.)*

■ *The wine industry in the US – like that in other countries – used to consist of a myriad of small independent vineyards, selling wine to a relatively small customer base through specialist distribution channels. There was little consumer branding. Companies like Gallo reasoned that instead of being an elitist product sold to connoisseurs, wine could reach a far larger market if it were treated like fast-moving consumer goods, reaping economies in production, distribution and marketing. They changed the face of their industry and expanded the market enormously.*

Once again, drawing analogies between one industry and another cannot be expected to produce ideas which can automatically be transferred. Many of the new ideas thrown up will simply be inappropriate; there are usually good reasons why industries work in one particular way rather than another. It can, however, do two things. Firstly, it can help generate ideas which might otherwise be missed. Secondly, and perhaps even more importantly, it can act as a catalyst to force management to think in creative and inquiring ways. Tom Peters describes this process as 'creative swiping'. To be valuable, it has to go beyond mere copying. It should act as a source of insights and as a catalyst for creativity.

Unexplained successes and failures

Unexplained phenomena – particularly successes – are often overlooked. As described by Peter Drucker in his book *Innovation and Entrepreneurship*,* they can provide valuable insights. Unexplained phenomena are not random occurrences, something to be put on one side and forgotten. They have a fundamental significance. It is this: we all operate with a conceptual map of how our industry works. It enables us to understand and predict behaviour. When it fails to do so (i.e. we have unexplained successes or failures) then the conceptual map is no longer valid. We no longer fully understand how the industry and our customers really work. We need a new conceptual map. Developing one is a challenging but rewarding process. When we have one which helps us to understand what is really going on, we have made a major step forward: we have built a new picture of what drives customer behaviour. That can be the first step in developing new ways of delivering customer value. It is therefore the first step in innovation (Figure 10). (Chapter 13 gives a fuller discussion of conceptual maps.)

Too many firms ignore these unexplained phenonema – particularly the successes. By so doing, they are letting valuable opportunities slip by. Opportunities to develop a deeper understanding of how their business works. Opportunities to innovate. Managers need to have the intellectual curiosity to pursue these inconsistencies until they are fully resolved. Once again, the benefits of so doing are two-fold: firstly there is the chance of unearthing some specific opportunity, and secondly it helps force the thinking into the right inquisitive, creative track. It improves one's understanding of one's own business. It helps generate individual innovations as well as developing a broader innovativeness. (See Chapter 12, Innovations and Innovativeness).

- *Roy Bishko had a small chain of heel bars in central London. He occasionally tried selling additional products through these outlets. Racks of inexpensive silk ties proved to be an unexpected success. Shortly afterwards he set up Tie Rack.*

- *The first computers were designed for scientific applications, not for business users. IBM displayed its first computer in its Madison Avenue showrooms. It calculated phases of the moon. Interest in buying the computer came from an unexpected quarter: companies which wished to*

Peter F. Drucker, Innovation and Entrepreneurship (Heinemann, 1985).

Figure 10: The value of unexplained successes and failures is that they can help us to develop a new, more creative and productive conceptual map.

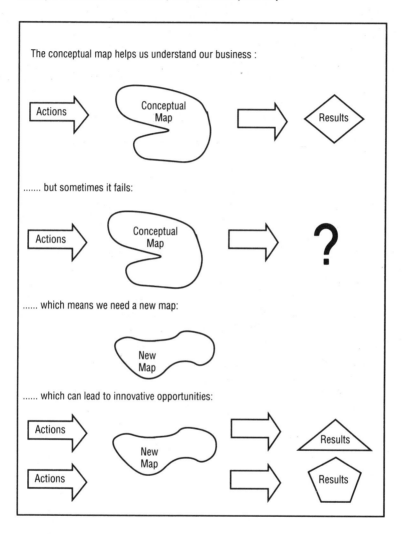

automate their payrolls. IBM – although surprised by the interest – responded enthusiastically. Univac remained aloof from the commercial market – even though its computer was more advanced than IBM's and more suited to business uses. This cost Univac dear – within four years IBM had become the clear leader in the computer industry.

- *A US company providing typesetting equipment to the newspaper and publishing industries noticed that it did far better with some customer groups than others. Closer examination showed this to be due to the distinct product and service needs of different emerging customer segments, whose needs were diverging ever more rapidly. They were subsequently able to develop product and service offerings tailored for each segment, and improved their performance in both.*

Technological limits and enabling changes

Some innovations depend upon a technological advance. The core concept of the innovation may have little to do with technology, but a technological advance is needed to deliver the new value to customers. Sometimes there are technological limits which prevent this from happening, and the innovative idea has to wait for some enabling change to take place before it can become a reality.

- *Selling insurance products direct to the public rather than via an intermediary has in principle many attractions for the insurer. The intermediary's commission is avoided, and the insurer has far greater control over the customer base. Information can be collected which enables the company to cross-sell additional products more effectively, as well as to make better underwriting and pricing decisions. In addition, this information can help focus the marketing effort more precisely, and so lead to economies in this part of the cost structure.*

    The problem historically has always been that it has cost the insurance company as much or more to sell the insurance itself as it saves by avoiding the intermediary's commission. It has also been extremely difficult in practice to use the additional information effectively. The ability to manipulate and analyse huge amounts of data at low cost has simply been unavailable. Direct selling thus conferred little or no advantage (Figure 11). As a result, attempts to do it met with only limited success.

    In recent years advances in information technology have changed all this. The application of information technology to the selling operation – from analysis of target markets on an ever more segmented basis, to its use in improving the effectiveness of the telephone sales operation – have brought down the average cost of selling a policy to well below the comparable commission level. Modern technology can also enable the insurer to deliver a more caring, personalized service. Massive reductions in the cost of computer memory and processing power have

Figure 11: There are advantages to selling certain insurance products direct to the customer. Historically, these advantages have been difficult to realize, however. Advances in information technology are now enabling insurers to unlock the source of added value.

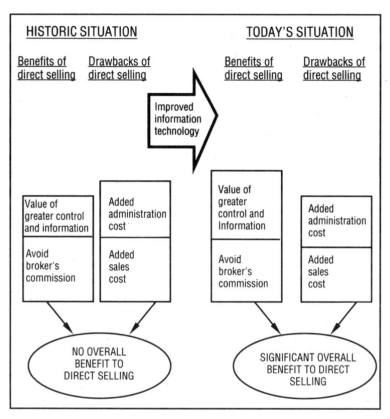

made it much more practical to utilize the additional control and information which direct selling can provide. This leads to significant improvements in price realization and claims experience, as the insurer targets individual segments more accurately. The overall effect is that the benefits of direct selling now far outweigh the drawbacks. This innovative approach is now a reality. Several companies are now engaged in a race to establish a leading position in this growing market. (Interestingly, the leading competitor is not a traditional insurance company, but a bank. It came at the problem afresh. It had fewer preconceived ideas of how insurance should be sold, and no entrenched position to protect.)

One of the key lessons to draw from this example is that innovation is not to do with technology per se. It is about customer service. The advances in information technology have merely ennabled the idea to achieve its full potential.

- *In a similar vein, Benetton's whole strategy is based upon colour and a rapid response to fashion changes and other feedback from the market. For this to work in practice, however, requires a sophisticated communications and computer system which links the retail outlets to the factory. Accurate and up-to-date information on the daily sales of every single product are fed back to the centre for incorporation into the design programme and manufacturing schedule. It requires the latest in flexible manufacturing technology. This enables the company to keep their shops stocked with fast moving merchandise, yet minimize their investment in working capital and the cost of having obsolete stock.*

- *USA Today has been a phenomenal success. Its basic concept was to provide the first truly national American newspaper with plenty of human interest editorial coverage and liberal use of colour. Until recently the Wall Street Journal was the only national daily. USA Today is particularly attractive to readers travelling far from home who may be unfamiliar with the local newspapers available in the area.*
  The concept was straightforward. Its implementation, however, required exploiting a number of technologies in colour, data communications and flexible printing technology. Without these, it would have remained a mere concept, instead of being the most succcessful new newspaper ever launched.

- *There is nothing new about technological limits. Leonardo da Vinci's notebooks are full of amazingly advanced ideas – parachutes, submarines, helicopters. None could be converted into reality until the limits – economic and social as well as technological – were removed.*

Perhaps the most significant aspect of such enabling changes is the time lag which is often involved. A technological advance in one field may make innovation possible in some apparently unrelated area. But it may be several years before it is realized and exploited. The reason is clear: when a technological advance does occur, the processes of communication and consideration of how it can be adapted simply take time. Once the full implications of the advance have been widely recognized, however, it is almost too late: several competitors are likely to be pursuing the same opportunity. What is needed is some way to gain a lead on the competition, to spot early on the technological changes which bring with them innovative opportunities.

The best way of doing this is to identify where the technological limits in the industry lie. A useful exercise is to brainstorm and generate a list of potential innovations which would be attractive to the consumer – a 'wish list'. One can then identify what technological advances would be needed in which areas for these innovations to become realistically possible. Often the key constraint is the ability to provide certain functions at an acceptable cost level (as in the insurance example above.) Quite often one finds that it is in one or two technological areas that most of the constraints lie. These are the critical ones to watch. Developments in these areas should be carefully monitored and their implications explored. The perspective should at all times be practical: how can this particular advance be of value in our business? Does it remove constraints? If this is done conscientiously and intelligently, then there is a very good chance that one can realize the implications of a new development well before one's competitors. The payoff can be tremendous: the firm can move from reaction to anticipation. It is a good idea to incorporate this analysis into the annual planning cycle. Each year progress in removing constraints should be monitored to see whether certain innovative moves are now possible. Sometimes it goes the other way, of course: new constraints can arise in place of older ones. Whichever way it goes, the firm which keeps an active watching brief on these developments has a valuable edge over the competition.

Discontinuities

Discontinuities take place from time to time in any industry. They include major legislative changes, the emergence of new competitors and customer needs and other fundamental events, in addition to the technological advances described above. Without exception they create opportunities. There are usually losers from such changes, but there are always gainers too. The real winners are those who can spot and exploit the implications before the competition. The true opportunities are often caused by some knock-on effect, rather than the discontinuity itself. Finding these opportunities requires an analysis which delves beyond the immediately apparent implications. Many major innovations arose out of such discontinuities:

■ *People Express grew rapidly in the 1970s and early 1980s in the deregulated US airlines market. The new environment allowed it to offer a fundamentally different package of services to anything seen before, and to deliver this with a radically different cost structure to that of any of its competitors. This package was the logical result of a new set of beliefs on customer behaviour and the economics of running an airline: there are potential customers who want basic transportation without any frills; focusing exclusively on their needs will yield major cost savings. Deregulation made it all possible. The availability of cheap secondhand aircraft and landing slots at inexpensive airports made it a reality.*

■ *The British government's introduction of the '25 per cent rule', whereby the BBC and ITV should commission a quarter of their programmes from independent producers, will obviously create a lot of opportunities for these companies. More than that, the rapid change resulting in the independent sector will in itself produce additional opportunities elsewhere – for facilities houses, focused service companies and so on. Many of the knock-on opportunities have yet to be identified as the changes filter through the whole broadcasting and production industry.*

■ *Television has had a profound influence on society. The drawback of broadcast television has always been that the economics of distribution have forced programme suppliers to cater for a mass audience. The arrival of multi-channel broadband cable in the US suddenly changed those economics. It became possible for innovators to focus complete channels on the needs of distinct target audiences. Several of these have gone on to become major businesses. Home Box Office, for example, provides recent films to some 19 million subscribers. Its turnover has passed $900 million.*

Discontinuities change the business environment. By their very nature they produce opportunities for innovation. This is generally acknowledged. Unless they are very shortsighted, the competitors will also be considering these opportunities. There is rarely much time to delay. Rapid and decisive action are paramount requirements for success. What is not always appreciated, however, is that sometimes the most significant effects may not be the direct ones, but knock-on effects in other parts of the industry. Careful thought and analysis is usually needed to identify these. It often pays off: it can take the firm into areas of opportunity where it can enjoy a significant lead over the competition.

Value chains

Innovation is fundamentally about understanding customers' needs. The acid test of any new concept must be whether or not it delivers added value to them. It is all too easy to fall into a particular set of assumptions as to what the customer really wishes and needs to buy. When this happens it puts a severe brake on innovative creativity. It is valuable to test the assumptions every so often. Michael Porter's value chain is a useful tool for investigating how markets work and how a firm's product or service interacts with its customers. Its potential value in the innovation process rests on the fact that it forces one to think through what it is that creates value for the customer. Understanding how one's own value chain interacts with that of one's customers (and, indeed, suppliers) is a vital step in considering how changes in what one does (i.e. changes in one's own value chain) can be of benefit to one's customers (i.e. how it effects their value chains.)

A value chain is nothing more than a diagrammatic representation of a firm's operations. It shows the major activities in each of several different areas, and the links which operate between them. The generic form of the value chain is shown in Figure 12.

Figure 12: The generic value chain displays the activities of the firm in a diagrammatic form.

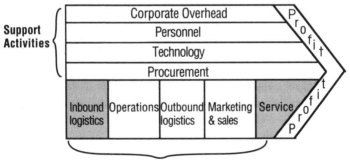

Primary activities

The firm's operations are divided into primary and support activites. The distinction between the two is straightforward: primary activities are those which have a direct bearing upon the product or service which the company supplies, while support activities are those staff functions which support the main line tasks.

The first stage in constructing a value chain is to identify the principal activities which fall into each of the categories in the generic chain. (For example specific steps in the manufacturing process would be listed in detail in the operations box.) Even in a small company, however, there will be too many individual activities for all of them to be listed in full: one has to concentrate on the major ones and include the less important ones alongside them. The criteria for choice should be firstly materiality – how significant the activity is in terms of cost, and secondly how those costs behave – one should collect together activities whose economics are determined by similar factors. For instance, the cost of some activities might depend on the firm's overall scale, while the cost of others could be determined by batch sizes.

The value chain is now complete, albeit in qualitative form. The next task is to quantify each of the individual activities in terms of their proportion of the total cost structure. This is difficult enough for one's own company – it is much more so when estimating one's customers' value chains and cost structures. Fortunately, approximate numbers are often adequate. The key objective is to develop a clear picture of how one's customer's business works, and think through quite carefully which are the high cost and value activities within it. The value chain's real worth lies in identifying and quantifying the links which exist between various operations within the firm, and between the firm and its customers and suppliers. (For example, how does product design influence failure rate? How does delivery time impact the value for the customer?) This is also the most difficult part to do properly. Anyone can split up a firm's operations into groups and estimate the cost of each. Correctly identifying the links between different operations is more difficult. It requires a relentless, probing approach to understanding the business: if we change this input, what happens elsewhere in the chain? The value chain forces one to be ruthlessly logical in analysing of the business. Understanding the links can often provide the key to major innovative opportunities:

- *Worm gears are used to provide large reduction ratios in many industrial applications. The market leader in a particular country had supplied a full range for decades. It offered 115 different ratio pairs in 11 different sizes. Those were the standards – other models were available to special order. Competitors' ranges were similar.*

  Its manufacturing operations were a mess. With production split between so many different models, the volumes of each one were tiny. Ten units was quite a large batch – many models were made in twos and threes. The firm didn't have a factory so much as a bespoke workshop.

It had in the past considered slimming down its range. Customers had flexibility in the ratios which they used: 98 per cent of their needs could in theory be met with only 30 different ratio pairs. How much volume would be lost in practice, however? Would customers switch to the products of competitors? The company compared the perceived risks of lost volume with what it considered to be the major benefit from the move: greater control over the manufacturing operation. Every time they performed the analysis the answer was the same: the risks outweighed the benefits. They maintained their unmanageable product range.

Recently they tackled the problem using the value chain analysis. This provided major insights into the likely value to be gained by narrowing the product range. The immediate effect was that the manufacturing operation would need to produce far fewer batches per month, but each batch would be individually larger. That this alone would simplify operations in the factory was no news to the company; they already knew this would happen. What the value chain analysis achieved was to help identify a whole range of indirect effects of moving to a narrower range. Their combined effect was a significant improvement in the firm's overall operations (Figure 13).

★ *With fewer product variants and larger production batches, both the raw materials and the finished goods operations were simplified (inbound and outbound logistics). This improved the firm's stock turn and ensured that a higher proportion of products were available from stock.*

★ *The improved stock turn reduced the company's working capital requirements, releasing a large amount of cash.*

★ *With a smaller range of parts to be purchased in individually larger volumes, the whole procurement operation was simplified. Small but worthwhile clerical staff savings were made.*

★ *With fewer, but larger batches, the company's labour requirements were altered. Fewer (highly paid) machine setters were needed, and were replaced by (less expensive) turners.*

★ *Failure rates declined drastically as batch sizes increased. This not only had a major beneficial effect on costs but also led to greater product reliability and reduced service needs.*

Figure 13: The immediate effect of a narrower product range would be in the firm's manufacturing operations

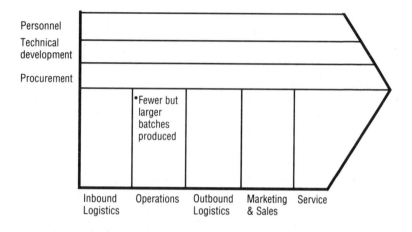

. . . but the knock-on effects for other areas of the firm's activities would be even more significant.

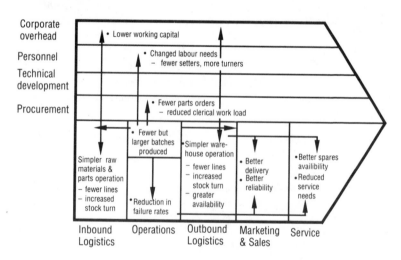

> ★ *The greater product reliability and improved delivery (since most items could now be carried in stock) made the sales and service departments' task a great deal easier.*

Even more important than the internal benefits, however, were the improvements which resulted in the firm's dealings with its suppliers and customers (Figure 14).

★ *The move to fewer but larger batches meant that the firm could give larger, more regular orders to its suppliers. The suppliers reaped economies from this, and could pass on part of the benefit in the form of a discount.*

★ *The firm's customers enjoyed better delivery and superior product reliability. Interviews with customers confirmed that this was a major benefit, more than offsetting any potential drawbacks from the move to a narrower range.*

Figure 14: The changes to the product range had major implications for both the firm's customers and its suppliers.

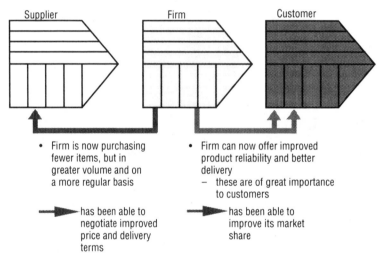

* Firm is now purchasing fewer items, but in greater volume and on a more regular basis

➤ has been able to negotiate improved price and delivery terms

* Firm can now offer improved product reliability and better delivery
  − these are of great importance to customers

➤ has been able to improve its market share

The overall effects were strongly positive: the narrower range would be of major benefit to the company, its customers and its suppliers. They implemented the change rapidly and successfully. Far from leading to any loss of volume, the improved delivery and reliability actually helped the firm to gain *market share.*

The narrower range was an innovative solution to the firm's problems. The idea had been mooted several times before, but had never amounted to anything. It took the value chain analysis to unlock the innovation and make it real. All of this can be done without a value chain, of course.

Most successful business people have a deep innate understanding of how their own and their customers' companies work and where the opportunities for leverage lie within their operations. What the value chain does is to provide a structure which forces one to think through these issues. If it is approached conscientiously it almost always provides new and potentially important insights into one's customers' operations. By itself it can produce nothing; it needs to be applied with intelligence and sensitivity.

The completed value chain provides a framework within which to consider how one's own product or service affects one's customers' operations. It provides the most appropriate context within which to pose and answer a number of questions, such as:

- What tradeoffs does the customer make between cost and performance? (e.g. Is a reduction in failure rate of 20 per cent worth a 10 per cent price premium? How would it affect the customer's economics?)
- What constitutes 'value' for the customer: reliability? delivery? service? etc. How well does our offering suit the customer's needs?
- Is it possible for us to provide a broader range of the inputs needed for the customer's value chain? A narrower range?
- Would it be worthwhile for us to integrate forward and take on some of the value added functions which the customer currently performs on our product? (e.g. Instead of selling components should we provide sub-assemblies?) Would there be overall system benefits to doing this? Conversely, should we provide the product or service in a less refined form?
- Do different customers have markedly different value chains – i.e. is there a distinct customer segmentation? How should we reflect this in our offering?

The value chain's worth is that it forces these questions out into the open, and helps address them. It is a convenient way to direct one's thinking onto the central issue of innovation: how to deliver new customer value.

CLOSING THE LOOP

None of the above approaches can by themselves guarantee success. They have to be viewed in the context of the firm's overall innovation efforts. Their value is two-fold:

- **Specific:** they provide a comprehensive checklist of places and ways to look for new ideas. They help to generate individual innovation ideas for evaluation.

- **Environmental:** they force management's thinking on to the right creative wavelengths. They help build the innovative environment which is needed.

Institutionalizing these approaches can be very useful; the more they become part of management's regular review and strategic planning cycle, the more they begin to influence the culture. This can be an incredibly powerful by-product over and above any specific innovations which they generate per se.

SUMMARY

The search for innovation relies on insight, creativity and luck. these are not random. They are amenable to management, which can be effective at two levels:

- **Environmental** level: improving the innovative environment within the company:
  - culture and beliefs
  - organization structure
  - personnel management

- **Specific** level: actions which can help to generate individual innovative opportunities:
  - analysis of **macro trends**
  - **translation** of ideas from one market to another
  - **analogy** with other industries
  - analysis of **unexplained successes**
  - consideration of **technological limits** and **enabling changes**
  - **discontinuity** management
  - analysis of one's own and one's customers' **value chains**.

The more the specific actions can become engrained and institutionalized, the more they begin to improve the innovative environment within the firm.

- The two levels should be pursued in parallel.

5   EVALUATING THE OPPORTUNITY

The evaluation method used has a profound influence on how successfully a company innovates. The approaches used in most firms are inadequate. The same method is often employed for fundamental innovations as for cost reductions and other low risk investments. They rely too heavily on financial information and ignore the key strategic issues. They are biased against true innovation and are poor at separating winners from losers.

They also fail to fulfil one of the evaluation's most vital roles: the ability to contribute to the strategy development process itself. A better approach is needed.

5 EVALUATING THE OPPORTUNITY

- The role of the evaluation

- Tight financial evaluation

- People-led evaluation

- Choosing a better way

- Evaluating innovations

THE ROLE OF THE EVALUATION

Whenever an innovative opportunity arises, it must be evaluated. However the idea has been developed, there comes a point at which the critical go / no go decision has to be made. Resources are needed to pursue the opportunity. For the individual entrepreneur or small company, finance must be raised from investors. In the large company, approval for the new idea must be given by top management or shareholders, and resources must be made available for it.

There must be almost as many systems for evaluating projects as there are companies. The methods used reflect the company's individual style, and cover a wide spectrum:

- Some companies follow hunches which management feel are worth backing, without engaging in long or detailed analysis.

- Others tend to back individual managers with track records, rather than focusing on the innovative idea itself. Implicitly their approach recognizes the importance of the management behind the new venture, sometimes ascribing a higher importance to this than to the detail of the idea itself.

- Many engage in more detailed financial analysis, judging the investment on the basis of payback period, discounted cash flow

(DCF), and the impact the investment is projected to have on the company's reported accounts.

- Still others adopt a more strategically focused approach, attempting to predict the impact of the investment on the firm's market share and, more generally, competitive position within the market in question.

Each method has its strong and weak points. What should concern us here is how the evaluation method chosen can influence both the success with which the company will tend to innovate, and also the type of innovation which is likely to be made. For it is an indisputable fact that different evaluation methods do tend to favour particular types of investment project – in many cases almost irrespective of the fundamental attractiveness of the opportunity itself. Before settling upon a particular method, therefore, firms should be aware of the likely directional implications of their choice. Indeed, choosing the most appropriate evaluation method is one of the more important actions which top management can take in order to steer their company's innovative efforts in the right directions.

TIGHT FINANCIAL EVALUATION

Before proposing an evaluation method which fosters innovation, it is worthwhile considering the more common methods used and exploring their implications. One of the most popular approaches – and particularly within large companies – is what one might call tight financial evaluation. A typical investment proposal might consist of a brief description of the opportunity and how it will be exploited, followed by a detailed financial analysis of how the new business is projected to perform. Typically this might consist of the following analyses:

- Projected profit and loss statements over, say, a five- or ten- year period.

- Cash flow projections, showing the annual and cumulative position, as well as the maximum total outflow. This indicates the funding requirement.

- Return on assets for the new business.

- A discounted cash flow (DCF) analysis. This discounts future costs and revenues into an equivalent amount in terms of today's money. It does this by allowing for the effects of compound interest, and can provide a number of measures of the attractiveness of the business. Most typically these are:

  - The net present value (NPV) of the cash flows from the project: by how much do the (discounted) revenues exceed the (discounted) investments?

  - The internal rate of return (IRR) of the project, which effectively shows the rate of return earned on the funds invested.

- A sensitivity analysis, showing what the effect would be on profitability, cash flow and return on assets of various changes to the original assumptions. Such changes might be higher or lower sales volumes, changes to prices or costs, or a longer or shorter period of investment required to develop the business. As the name suggests, it provides management with an idea of how the investment is likely to perform if their original assumptions are invalid for one reason or another.

Once submitted, the plan is subject to scrutiny largely on the basis of this financial analysis. Many firms have a 'hurdle rate' for return on assets or IRR, below which they will not support a new project. In one form or another these investment appraisal methods have been in use in large companies for a generation. Most significantly, the same type of investment appraisal is often used to evaluate widely differing types of project – from cost reductions on existing production lines to innovative new ventures.

In order to consider how this type of appraisal method works in practice for innovations, let's look back at our original definition of innovation: new ways of delivering customer value. By its very nature, a significant innovation changes the way in which the market operates. This holds irrespective of whether it is a fundamentally new product, a new way of distributing goods or services, a change in production methods or some other way of satisfying newly emerging customer needs. Whichever one it is, it almost always entails a high degree of uncertainty. Indeed, the more fundamental the innovation (and hence potentially the more rewarding in the long term) the greater will be the uncertainty. This uncertainty covers both sides of the profit and loss statement:

- **Costs:** the investment required to get an innovation to the market is always extremely uncertain. Changes are frequently required to the original concept, absorbing both time and resources. Customers may accept the new idea more quickly or more slowly than was anticipated. It is almost axiomatic that major innovations will take longer and cost more to develop than expected.

   ■ *Philippe Le Roux describes Norton's experiences along the way to getting its revolutionary rotary engines ready for and accepted by major users in the unmanned military aircraft field: 'The whole task took two years instead of one. Every single change takes longer than one thinks: a changed part needs four or five new drawings, not one. Each one has to go through the drawing office – and they have to make sure it is the latest drawing which is being altered and not a previous version. The parts orders then have to be progressed through the purchasing department, which secures at least three quotes. Occasionally when the parts come back there is a further design or quality problem. We are now on our third version of the engine, the "C-series". This is the version we have now taken into production.'*

   ■ *This is an almost universal experience among innovators, and is well known to venture capitalists. Adrian Beecroft of Alan Patricof Associates comments: 'It is commonly thought that when you have an idea which customers like, then you are home and dry. Nothing could be further from the truth. For example, customers love the in-situ car servicing offered by AutoMek. (This services customers' vehicles at their own premises, saving them the time and inconvenience of driving to the garage.) Even though it is a relatively simple concept, it has taken several years to be perfected. In the process it has changed from being a franchise operation to full ownership – primarily for quality control – and the original entrepreneur has left the business.'*

- **Revenue:** innovative ideas and products must offer customers tangible benefits. While the innovator should have a clear concept of the nature of the benefit, in many cases its precise value to the customer is uncertain. Even more importantly, many innovations provide benefits – initially at least – to some segment rather than to the whole market. The size of that segment is often an unknown proportion of the whole market and, moreover, one which may well grow over time as the innovation becomes more refined. These facts often make the size of the potential market and the speed with which it can be developed extremely difficult to determine. Two examples may help to illustrate this:

■ *Norton's rotary engines have many advantages relative to either two-or four-stroke reciprocating engines. They have an unequalled power-to-weight ratio, low vibration, good reliability and longevity, and a fuel consumption equivalent to a four-stroke (and far superior to a two-stroke). In addition they are far simpler than competing engines, having fewer moving parts. In principle they have great potential in almost all applications where internal combustion engines are currently used: automotive, marine, aviation, generators etc. One outstanding question remains: production cost. At present they are made in small numbers, and therefore at a relatively high cost. The engine's ability to penetrate the high volume applications – which should eventually be the really major payoff for Norton – is largely contingent upon how costs will decline over time. That is an unknown as yet. What Norton is doing today – with great success – is to penetrate first those applications where the engine's distinctive performance characteristics are of the greatest value. Hence the company's focus on airborne and military applications, where power-to-weight ratio and vibration are particularly important. At present it is extremely difficult to be more specific about the potential in the higher volume applications, other than to say that it is very large. Try putting that into a DCF calculation!*

■ *Scetlander is a Glasgow-based educational software publisher that has adopted an innovative approach to its industry. It has a joint venture structure which brings together the complementary commercial and educational skills of its two partners (Scotlander plc and the Scottish Council for Educational Technology, SCET). By so doing, the company has gained access to a low cost source of tried and tested software and also better access to distribution channels than its competitors. For an initial period of five years it has exclusive rights to all new software produced by SCET. Like many start-up companies, however, the scope of the opportunity was far from clear when it started. Ron Lander describes the situation: 'Our first year and a half was effectively a period of research and experimentation – we had to explore not only the market but also the ways in which the joint venture could function most effectively, and to build up contacts in educational establishments internationally. We have built a trained team, have established a customer base (which includes two thirds of all the local authorities in the country) and are now in a position to start selling in earnest. An equivalent programme of market research by outsiders would have cost a fortune – and would not have provided the same depth of information or contacts.'*

Consider now how significant innovations like the above ones would fit into most companies' financial evaluation systems. Costs, revenues and time estimates are extremely uncertain. The key considerations in evaluating any significant innovation should clearly be the strategic ones:

- What is the new value that is being created?

- For whom?

- How will it be delivered (i.e. implemented)?

The financial evaluation process however, positively diverts attention away from these considerations, and focuses instead on the numbers. Instead of *reflecting* the reality of the business situation, the numbers *replace* it. They become the focus of attention, in place of the innovative idea itself. The numbers are by their very nature uncertain in the extreme – yet they are needed to fit into the evaluation process. So the innovator picks some reasonable projections and puts forward his case.

Now compare the innovative idea with, say, a cost reduction or capacity expansion proposal in a well established part of the business. The latter will have more hard data and far less uncertainty. Beside it the innovation will appear at best highly uncertain and at worst extremely questionable. It will be full of what appear to be rather arbitrary and dangerous assumptions. It will be easy to pick holes in it. Now, which project is the more likely to be approved?

Financial analysis is extremely valuable and has a valid role to play in evaluating new opportunities. Taken to extremes, however, it has two very strong and often undesirable implications:

- It **focuses attention on the numbers themselves**, and away from the underlying strategic business realities. It completely ignores a vital aspect of evaluation: the opportunity to probe and test the hypotheses and logic behind the evaluation. Instead, it provides merely a 'yes' or 'no' decision.

- It predisposes towards low risk, marginal investments, and **positively discourages major innovations**.

An exclusively financially-focused approach to evaluating new ventures can not only inhibit the mature company's innovative success – it can also place the company's base business in danger:

■ *Consider the case of a well established financial services group that was a leader in its field. It had correctly identified the likely emergence of a major shift in the distribution channels for its product. The new channel would offer lower costs, superior service and far better control over the customer base. Within a few years it was quite likely that a large proportion of the market would have gone over to the new distribution channel.*

The firm evaluated a venture based on the new channel. Knowledge of the new business was scarce, but financial projections and evaluations were done. The payback period and DCF calculation showed only a relatively mediocre return: a large proportion of sales volume gained in the new channel would be won at the expense of the firm's existing business. The firm very nearly did not go ahead with the investment – yet not to have done so would have forfeited a potentially pivotal part of the market to more innovative competitors. And all this based on a set of financial projections which relied upon patchy information in the first place! The firm had evaluated the opportunity in exactly the same way in which it might judge an investment in some area completely unrelated to its base business. In reality, however, the firm had no choice. The new distribution channel was going to become increasingly important: they could either enter it or accept the long-term loss of a major part of their business.

PEOPLE-LED EVALUATION

The drawbacks of a purely financially-led investment appraisal process have been recognized and commented on before. While most large companies soldier on with them, however, there has recently been something of a trend away from such methods. Investors and senior management increasingly recognize the importance of having the right people involved in a project, and then managing and motivating them in the right way. Some large companies have adopted people-led appraisal methods for their corporate venturing programmes. They pursue those ventures which have the enthusiastic backing of a manager with a strong track record. They implicitly make a number of assumptions:

● **Product champion:** one of the most important factors in the success of any new venture is that there should be a strong 'champion' involved, who is committed to the new business.

- **Track record:** if a manager has a strong track record in one part of the corporation, then he will probably do well in the task of building up a new venture.

This recognition of the importance of the individual to the new venture is entirely laudable. Focusing on this to the exclusion of the strategic realities, however, is not. This is true for several reasons:

- **Strategic:** the best manager in the world will not succeed with a new concept which does not deliver new customer value. If the proposed innovation does not do this, it will fail. Likewise, the wrong management team will cripple the soundest business concept. Both aspects must be right before the business will grow successfully; all venture capitalists recognize this.

  The real danger inherent in focusing exclusively on the people involved is that it diverts attention from the strategic realities of the business itself. Although it is attractive and easy for investors or senior management to back individuals rather than to analyse the strategic detail of a new business idea, it simply will not work. Too many innovations fail and too many managers with previously good track records get involved with them for such a hands-off approach to succeed. The evaluation process simply must get down into the strategic detail of the business.

- **Strategy development:** even if it were possible to delegate consideration of the strategic detail to the line managers of the new venture, to do so would be extremely dangerous. A strategy which has not been laid out in black and white is almost always an unclear strategy. It is only too easy to brush over inconsistencies and invalid assumptions in a strategy which has not been made explicit. The need to communicate – and defend – a strategy is an extremely useful discipline. It forces the thinking up to a new level. Making strategy explicitly a part of the investment appraisal process not only serves to weed out the losing ideas, but also strengthens the winners. The evaluation should do more than just provide a 'yes' or 'no' decision. It should be a central part of the strategy development process: by asking the right questions it can ensure that the business proceeds on the basis of a carefully thought out, watertight strategy.

- **Different skills:** a manager's success in a previous role is actually no guarantee that he will do well at starting a new venture. The key tasks and skills differ markedly for companies at different phases of their development. The type of manager needed changes too. For example, very few entrepreneurs stay with their company as it grows to maturity. Leading venture capital firms recognize this, and install professional management to complement the skills of the entrepreneur at an early stage.

- **Control:** finally, concentrating on the individual rather than on the detail of the business idea results in a great loss of control for the firm. In some situations the firm will generate and pursue too few new opportunities, in others too many. Additionally, the firm can easily lose control over the direction in which it is innovating.

CHOOSING A BETTER WAY

Neither the financially-oriented nor the people-oriented evaluation methods have proved to be very successful. If they were, corporate venturing would be a great success. By and large, it is not. The first method tends to result in too conservative an approach to innovation, while the latter often leads to too many ideas being pursued, in too unfocused a manner. Something else is required.

Ideally, the evaluation should fulfill a number of objectives and, specifically, should avoid the shortcomings of the traditional methods as described above. The features which it should have are:

- **Strategic focus:** it should concentrate above all on the nature of the innovation itself. In other words it should adopt a strategic focus, containing a full description of the innovation: just how it delivers new customer value, and for whom.

- **Strategy development:** many innovative ventures fail for lack of a focused strategy. The value of introducing a carefully thought-out strategy at an early stage is inestimable. Rather than simply providing a go/no go decision, it would be more useful if the evaluation method could provide some positive feedback into the strategy development process.

- **Uncertainty:** it should reflect and cope with the uncertainty inherent in innovative ideas. Proposals should not be heavily penalized for the degree of uncertainty surrounding them, nor should the evaluation require unrealistic and misleading levels of detail.

- **Flexibility:** it should recognize that most major innovations will evolve significantly between the initial concept and their final form. Exploring innovative ideas will often open up completely new avenues which were not even considered initially. The evaluation method should have the flexibility to accommodate this.

- **Financial:** finally, the evaluation method must of course reflect the basic commercial realities. It would be incomplete without analysis of the likely cash requirements and potential profitability.

In order to incorporate these requirements into an evaluation procedure one further observation is appropriate. It is a statement of belief, but one which is strongly borne out by experience:

- If the concept behind a proposed venture does encompass some new way of delivering customer value (i.e. is truly innovative) then it will be possible to build a business around the innovation. The precise form of the business and how it can be built up and run may not be clear at this point, but will become so as time progresses and more is discovered about the opportunity. The key factor for consideration must be whether the new concept really can deliver new customer value – not whether a particular set of financial assumptions gives a positive or a negative result.

Realistically, this means that many successful innovations must proceed first in a fact-finding mode, without a full understanding of how they will develop later on, or even of the full extent of the opportunity. It is necessary, however, that the experimentation and learning should be done in a fully commercial environment – i.e. it should be a trial launch of the business itself, not an elaborate programme of market research. Funding research can be of great value to any business, but there comes a point – and normally sooner rather than later – when research is unable to answer the really important questions: will it really cost x to produce this component? Must the price be competitive with the existing service or can we charge a 10 per cent premium? Will we really be able to adapt the product to sell it to foreign customers? And so on. The only sure way to answer these questions and hundreds of others like them is to try them out. In practice there are very few business ideas for which the critical assumptions cannot be be tested out at a limited risk and cost. One of the most important aspects of succesfully starting innovative new ventures is to find ways of testing them at limited risk, but also without compromising the idea itself. Some of the most consistently innovative companies are masters at this:

■ *Kwik-Fit, the Edinburgh-based express tyre and exhaust fitter, modelled its innovation on the muffler shops which were established in the US by the late 1960s. Tom Farmer set it up using his own capital in one outlet in the UK in 1970. To the original service concept others have been added: Stop 'n' Steer, a specialist brake and steering service outlet, and Kwik Lube, a menu-based full service and M.O.T. outlet. Others are under consideration on an ongoing basis: specialized clutch outlets, panel repair outlets etc. In each case the concept is tested in full – but with limited cost and risk – by introducing it on a trial basis into a small number of existing outlets. If successful, it can be rolled out as a separate chain quite quickly. Tom Farmer describes the firm's approach: 'The original founders have quite frequent evening sessions to discuss the future direction of the group. Our overall goal is to dominate all aspects of car service, from purchase to the scrap yard. We never do anything because 'it's a good idea – let's give it a try': we always analyse and test it out in detail first. Not that we do big research studies or anything like that – we think it through and then thrash it out amongst ourselves, and then test it. For example, clutches will be tested in ten existing outlets to see how the idea works.'*

EVALUATING INNOVATIONS

The optimal evaluation process takes the above objectives into account. It is in fact a formalization of the methods which many innovative firms and entrepreneurs already use. It is designed to draw out the essential strategic points underlying the innovation and also to contribute actively to the formulation and implementation of the business plan.

The evaluation is centred on a concise statement of the strategy underlying the innovation. It is the strategic analysis of what the innovation is and does for the customer which should entail the greatest effort and receive the closest scrutiny within the evaluation. After all, it is upon this that the innovation will succeed or fail. It consists of five distinct steps:

- **Description of the business environment:** this should cover the market in which the innovation will take place in both quantitative and qualitative terms. It should give estimates of the overall market size and growth rate, and split this up into relevant definable segments. It should describe the distribution channels in some detail, again giving their relative sizes and growth rates. It should identify the relevant competitors, with estimates of their market shares, positionings, strengths and weaknesses. Most important of all, perhaps, it should qualitatively describe what is going on: how do customers behave? Why? What do they really need? How is the product or service provided? What are the strengths and weaknesses inherent in this system?

This stage may seem to be unnecessary – after all, we all know our own markets very well. To omit or skim over it can be extremely dangerous, however. It provides the necessary context and perspective for all the subsequent analyses. (One firm I know spent an inordinate amount of time and effort considering their strategy for a particular area which could constitute at most one per cent of their turnover. A little effort spent on this early stage would have saved a lot of time and trouble.)

- **Description of the innovation:** a brief but comprehensive description of the proposed concept. What will it change? Why will this be of value to the customer? What are the key hypotheses which underlie the innovation? How certain or uncertain are they? How can these hypotheses be tested? Which customers will receive most value from the innovation and why?

- **Strategic evaluation of the innovation:** the aim here is to attempt to quantify the added value which the previous section has defined. If the innovation's main effect is to save customers money, then what economies are actually involved? How much is saved at the *cost* level (as opposed to prices)? Does the saving vary for different types of customers or segments of the market? How large is each segment? If the main benefit is increased value to the customer rather than reduced cost, then how can that value be quantified? What analysis can be done, or what analogies can be drawn to show how customers will value the change to the product or service? Again, will the change be of equal benefit to all customers, or will some value it more highly than others? This analysis does more than just give an estimate of the potential market size for the innovation. It also shows which areas should be the first segments to be attacked.

  How easy or difficult will it be for competitors – either existing or potential – to replicate the innovation? What barriers to entry (real or perceptual) will there be? Will being first be an advantage or a disadvantage in the long term? More generally, how will competitors respond to the innovation? How long will it be before they are likely to respond, and what position will we be in by then?

What are the major uncertainties that still exist? How important are they to the fundamental viability of the innovation? How important are they to the extent of the value created for individual customer types?

- **Business plan:** how can the innovation be implemented? What are the different options? What do each of them require in the way of resources and time? When will the uncertainties be resolved, and what is the maximum cash which will have been expended at that point? What are the natural checkpoints along the way which will indicate how well or otherwise the venture is proceeding? At what point should we pull out if necessary? (Too many new ventures proceed with no clear checkpoints agreed. When things start to go wrong they can easily drift for months before taking decisive corrective action.) What are realistic projections of sales volumes over the foreseeable future? What is the most pessimistic but still reasonable projection of sales volume?

- **Financial evaluation:** if the potential for the innovation is sufficiently certain, then the standard financial analysis can be completed, giving projected profitability and a DCF calculation. If there is still significant uncertainty, then an analysis for each of the options identified in the previous section can be done, giving:

  - the cash outflows up to the point where the key uncertainties will have been resolved for better or for worse. This should give a best, a medium and a worst case.

  - Similarly, the cash inflows from the sales which are likely from the *most certain and immediately exploitable market segments* (i.e. the ones where there is relatively little uncertainty). In certain circumstances, of course, the answer to this may be 'zero': all revenues are far from certain or even highly probable. Again a best, medium and worst case should be projected.

  - Finally, some very broad-brush estimate must be made of the possible upside. Once the uncertainties have been resolved and assuming the innovation does give customers the added value which we hope, what sales and profit streams are possible? Again a best, medium and worst case should be projected.

What this evaluation method aims to achieve is four-fold:

- Instead of treating an innovative opportunity in the same way as, say, a simple cost reduction investment, it makes the costs, risks and returns individually more visible. It does not try to reduce them to one simple – and therefore simply misleading – number such as NPV. It attempts to evaluate the investment required to resolve the uncertainties inherent in the venture.

- It focuses attention on the critical strategic issues surrounding the innovation. These are the questions which above all determine the success or failure of the venture. By concentrating attention upon them, it ensures that the evaluation is made upon the best basis possible. By doing so it enables better decisions to be made.

- This focus on the strategic issues forces the line managers involved in the project to make their strategy explicit. This alone is of major importance: it improves the quality of the strategy and the business plan. It increases the chances of success.

- By identifying the critical assumptions underlying the innovation it provides a natural series of checkpoints. If any assumptions are subsequently shown to be invalid this becomes immediately apparent. Top management can take appropriate action, limiting the company's exposure to loss.

The evaluation method is a powerful tool in helping to foster innovation within a corporation. There is perhaps no other single action that top management can take which has as immediate and lasting an effect. The principles are straightforward. In practice it requires effort: the strategic analysis of innovation has to be undertaken carefully to give valuable results. It is worthwhile. It can make a real difference.

SUMMARY

The evaluation method used does more than simply provide yes/no decisions:

- It should be an integral part of the innovation process itself.

Traditional investment appraisal and evaluation methods do not meet the needs of innovative companies well:

- They tend to penalize innovative opportunities.
- They provide no feedback to the strategy development process.

The ideal evaluation procedure for innovations has a fundamentally strategic focus. It has five stages:

- Description of the business environment
- Description of the innovation
- Strategic evaluation of the innovation
- Business plan
- Financial evaluation.

6 INVOLVING THE CUSTOMER

Involving customers in the innovation process increases the chances of success. It makes the innovation more relevant to customers' needs and makes them more likely to accept the new idea rapidly.

Few firms fully involve their customers. They are missing valuable opportunities.

6 INVOLVING THE CUSTOMER

- Customers: the ultimate asset

- Barriers to involvement
  - Credibility
  - Competitive risks

- To involve or not to involve?

CUSTOMERS: THE ULTIMATE ASSET

Customers are arguably any firm's greatest asset. They do not appear on the balance sheet, but nevertheless represent the true worth of the business. In most companies, however, the true value of the customer base is never fully exploited. This is particularly true as regards innovation. Involving customers intimately and early on in the innovation process can make all the difference between success and failure, yet few firms do. The advantages are significant:

- **Timing:** in many businesses there are certain isolated points in time at which customers can incorporate changes. It is at these points that they can benefit most from innovations. By involving them early on in the process, the chances of the new product or service coinciding with one of these points can be maximized:

  - *In the construction equipment business, for example, product lines might typically undergo major design and engineering changes every five to ten years. The design process itself might take three to five years. Suppliers of major components to the equipment manufacturers must ensure that their new product ideas fit in with these cycles. If they do not, then the customer (i.e. the equipment manufacturer) incurs extra costs to incorporate the change. There is a cost of switching. These costs detract from the value created by the innovation. Its value to the customer is diminished. At best, this reduced value must be passed back to the supplier in the form of lower prices. At worst, the customer is unable to use the innovation until the next major model change. This may mean a delay of several years.*

If, on the other hand, component changes can be introduced at the same time as the major model redesign, then the cost of incorporating them is lower. The innovation creates more value for the customer. It will be more successful (Figure 15).

Suppliers who involve their customers in their ideas for new products or services as early as possible have a major advantage. They can work with their customers to ensure that the innovation is incorporated into the equipment redesign programme. The more customers know about their suppliers' new ideas and the earlier they know them, the more they are likely to keep their options open, enabling them to design the innovation into their own product. Otherwise the supplier risks being frozen out until the next major model redesign.

Figure 15: Timing innovations correctly can reduce the cost of switching and so maximize the value created for the customer.

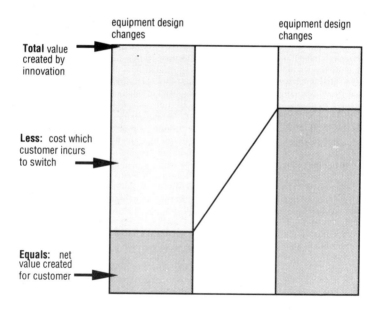

- **Positioning:** the simple psychology of selling argues in favour of involving customers early on. The more they can contribute to the innovation process, the more emotionally committed they become to it. By the time the new product or service is ready for introduction to the market, the selling job has already been partly completed.

  ■ *There are several ways in which customers can be involved. At one extreme it can involve little more than keeping them fully abreast of the firm's developments. At the other extreme it can entail establishing joint ventures or other formal relationships. Elmjet is a young firm which is developing a new system for ink-jet printing. The system will provide non-impact printing, in colour, on a range of different materials, such as fabrics, carpets and wallpapers. It has set up cooperation agreements with five major potential users of the new system. They pay an annual fee, give Elmjet access to their facilities for testing and undertake joint development projects. In return they receive priority (but not exclusivity) in ordering any product that emerges. They also have an early view on how this potentially important new technology is developing.*

This argument can be extended to include involving customers indirectly through the salesforce. In many types of consumer market, for example, one of the most significant barriers to the success of a new product is the ability to gain access to distribution (Figure 16). The increasing pressure for supermarket shelf space means that only significantly novel products can gain adequate distribution. The retail trade has little need of me-too products. Research in the US shows that involving the sales force in the innovation process from an early stage can be a potent weapon which significantly shortens the odds of success. The sales force are in touch with the channels of distribution and are familiar with their needs. If they can feed this information into the innovation process, then they become partners in that process. Their commitment will be far greater once the product actually comes to launch.

- **Development:** few ideas are completely right the first time. Most require either marginal or even significant modification. Often several iterations are needed before the final and successful format is arrived at. The ability to deliver new customer value is the key determinant of that success. To exclude customers from the process is ridiculous. Involving them early on can save significant time and cost: not only can it cut out abortive attempts and get to the final solution more

Figure 16: Distribution can be a major barrier to new product development.

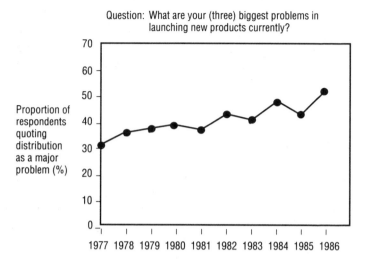

Question: What are your (three) biggest problems in launching new products currently?

Proportion of respondents quoting distribution as a major problem (%)

1977 1978 1979 1980 1981 1982 1983 1984 1985 1986

Source: **KAE Development Ltd**

quickly; it can also radically improve the match with customers' needs:

- ■ *The managing director of a small technology-based company comments: 'We are establishing relationships with these companies now so that we are not working in an ivory tower. Having them on board prevents us from developing something with a lefthanded fitting when what they want is a righthanded one.'*

- ● **Forcing the pace:** if customers are not involved in an innovation, progress usually seems to be slower than expected. There is always one aspect which needs further work before it is perfect. It can be very tempting to hold back from launching a new idea until every wrinkle has been ironed out. Left unchecked, this can become a serious distraction, diverting management from its central task of implementing the innovation and generating revenue. The new venture can degenerate into an extended research project, with no definite end in sight. As each problem is resolved, another one arises. The more the customer is involved, the less this is likely to happen. Their presence forces the pace for management: it is impossible to drift indefinitely without seriously damaging the firm's credibility. The benefits of involving customers extend beyond timing itself to include forcing a clearer focus on management. With deadlines agreed and set with customers, there is simply not time to spend on those interesting but marginal aspects of the innovation. All efforts must be focused on the really essential elements of the new concept to ensure that customers' expectations are met.

BARRIERS TO INVOLVEMENT

These and other considerations all favour involving the customer both early on and deeply in the innovation process. Yet, few firms do this. Why? While some may simply not have considered doing so, others may have contemplated it, but shied away for two principal reasons: credibility and competitive risks.

Credibility

Some managers appear to think that it is inappropriate to seek guidance from their customers. They believe that their customers look to them for advice and expertise, not the other way around. To ask for help in developing a new concept is thought to be an admission of weakness and unprofessional in some way. Worse, involving customers early on could damage the firm's credibility when the inevitable setbacks and rethinks occur.

In reality of course, little could be further from the truth. Very few customers are anything other than pleased and flattered to be consulted in detail on possible improvements to their supplier's product or service. Enlisting the customer's help in developing an innovation is highly professional; it communicates caring and empathy. It can only enhance the firm's standing. (For some companies it may require learning a little humility – but that is generally no bad thing either.)

■ *Bill Bowerman was an athletics coach at the University of Oregon in the 1950s. Like most other coaches he saw the existing athletic footwear as a serious impediment to improved performance. Unlike others, he did something about it. He ceaselessly experimented with new shoe designs tailored for individual athletes and events. Gradually he developed an approach to shoe design and construction which had a major impact on comfort and performance. (For example the waffle sole for running shoes was developed when Bill poured synthetic rubber into his wife's waffle iron.)*

Together with Phillip Knight, an ex-pupil, he set up Blue Ribbon Sports, later to become Nike. By 1985, Nike had become a billion dollar company and a clear market leader in all the major markets worldwide. From the outset it had a major advantage over the competition: it listened. The company's salesmen were all runners. They travelled to athletics meetings and talked with the sportsmen, listened to their problems. Nike rapidly developed a superior product range and a strong following among serious athletes. The jogging boom transformed it into a billion dollar company. All along the way, the ability to listen and learn paid dividends.

An early employee once commented: 'Our product, at the beginning, really was not that great. But I think we listened real well. We had come up from a background of using the other (competitors') products. Our competition had a 20-year head start on us. We'd worn all of their shoes, and we'd hurt, we had injuries. Bowerman was coming up with some neat ideas. He was taking mid-sole material and putting softer material up against our foot. He was experimenting with nylon uppers, and that was a lot more comfortable than leather. He began with a few small little things, and as you look back you don't think they're all that innovative, but back then they were pretty revolutionary.'

In 1986, Nike lost its market leadership of the US athletic footwear market to Reebok. According to Reebok's president, Joseph La Bonte, his company had 'analysed what they (aerobics fans) wanted from their sports shoes at a time when other manufacturers were run by sports jocks, who made the sort of shoes they liked themselves.' It found a rapidly growing niche: stylish soft leather shoes for aerobics. Nike, having listened so carefully to the needs of athletes and joggers, had failed to do the same for this rapidly emerging market segment. It paid the price.

Manufacturers worldwide are introducing elements of the Toyota Production System into their own factories. It calls for much closer links – indeed partnership – with their suppliers. The fundamental basis for the customer-supplier relationship is changing. The number of suppliers is being reduced in favour of closer relationships with each one. In this environment successful innovation will increasingly require communication and joint efforts between customers and suppliers.

It is, of course, important to position things appropriately. Rather than 'launching' a new idea the firm should get its customers to participate in a programme to develop the new concept. This immediately defuses the situation. Instead of selling the new idea to its customers, both parties are then working together to improve their mutual performance. Correctly handled, the potential risks involved in innovating can be markedly reduced. Moreover, this process can be a tremendous source of goodwill. Its benefits can extend far beyond the innovation itself to strengthen and deepen all the firm's relationships with its customers.

Competitive risks

Competitive risks are often cited as a reason for not involving customers in innovations. Involving any outsiders at all in the process introduces the risk that the lead may be lost to a rival. This is a legitimate concern: there are indeed situations where the risks are real and should be avoided.

The actual competitive risks are usually, however, far less than is normally thought to be the case. In industry after industry competitors have been seen to take far longer to respond to innovative initiatives than was ever anticipated. By the time the response does come, or the idea is copied, it is normally too late: the innovator has secured an unassailable lead:

- *Tie Rack was and is a beautifully simple concept. It would alter the whole way in which people think about and purchase ties, changing them into a fashion accessory bought on impulse. The company opened its first outlet in 1981. By the end of 1987 it had 152 outlets and an extremely profitable business – but no serious imitators.*

- *Federal Express Vice Chairman, Arthur Bass, describes how Emery (previously the market leader) could have killed off its new upstart competitor if it had acted early enough. It failed to do so – and lost the lead: 'In a fight between an alligator and a bear, the winner is determined not by ability but by the terrain – on land the bear wins, in the swamp the alligator wins. When we started out, Emery could have kicked the crap out of us, but didn't. Now it'll have to come into the swamp to fight us – and its not going to be any contest.'*

- *Arthur Jones, the founder of Nautilus exercise equipment, provides an insight into competitive behaviour as he describes how the established suppliers responded to his innovative approach: 'ignore, ridicule, attack, copy, steal'. By the time competitors get around to copying or stealing, however, it is usually too late.*

■ *Experienced venture capitalists recognize the slowness with which entrenched competitors usually respond. This factor alone often plays a major role in the success of innovative start-ups. Adrian Beecroft of Alan Patricof Associates describes his experience: 'Competitors are always slower to respond than one imagines they will be. In many cases the new player can establish a strong and secure position before he faces any real competitive response. This slowness on the part of the entrenched competitors is often the innovator's greatest asset.'*

TO INVOLVE OR NOT TO INVOLVE?

Although competitive response to innovation tends to be slow and ineffective, there are occasions where it can be blisteringly quick. New consumer electronics products are often copied within a matter of months. New fare structures or pricing initiatives on competitive air routes rarely go unmatched for long. Concern over such competitive risks is entirely legitimate. What is it that determines the speed and effectiveness of competitive response to an innovation? Even more importantly, how can one estimate the risk of a rapid response? And having estimated the risk, how can one best choose between involving customers fully, benefiting from their contribution but accepting the competitive risks, and maintaining secrecy as long as possible, thereby foregoing these benefits?

There are three principal considerations which should be borne in mind when evaluating whether or not to involve customers:

● **Head-on competition:** does any one competitor stand to lose a great deal from the innovation in the short term? How visible will it be to the competitors? Many innovations arise from targeting some customer segment in a completely new way. In situations like this the competitors will often at first not notice what is happening. Their attentions are directed at the overall market, not some segment of it. In these cases, the competitive risks are often low. It is where the innovation competes head-on and visibly with an existing competitor that the response is most likely to be rapid and effective.

- **Degree of novelty:** how innovative is the innovation? The more radical it is, the stronger the arguments are for involving customers fully in its development:

  - Their involvement is all the more valuable in such situations, since the inherent uncertainty is great and there is likely to be considerable freedom in the detailed definition of the new business within the overall concept. Customers' contributions can markedly increase the chances of success. They can also speed up the whole process: involving customers can often remove a whole stage from the process of getting the new idea right.

  - The risk of competitive response is lower. Competitors' first reactions to really radical innovation are almost certain to be dismissal and scorn, for the new idea runs counter to all their experience and intuition. It does not fit their conceptual maps. By the time they realize their mistake, it is often too late.

  Conversely, if the innovation represents only a marginal change from the existing situation (many new consumer product launches fall into this category), then the arguments for maintaining secrecy are stronger:

  - The innovation fits into the competitors' existing conceptual maps. They will rapidly recognize its significance and, if appropriate, respond.

  - Given that the new idea is not far from the firm's current experience, there is less uncertainty involved. Customers' contributions to the development process are arguably less critical than in truly radical innovations. Involving them is a lower priority.

- **Complexity:** how complex is the innovation in a business sense? Some – such as a new product design – are relatively straightforward and easy to copy (e.g. new consumer electronics products). For these the competitive risks are high: competitors can find out a great deal merely by taking the product apart. Others are much more complex, involving changes to several aspects of the business system (e.g. a new retail concept might involve changes in the product design, systems, manufacturing and distribution operations, as well as to the retail outlets themselves). These innovations are generally more difficult to copy, reducing the competitive risks:

■ *The Toyota Production System (Just-In-Time) has been developed continuously since the 1940s. The underlying concept is relatively simple. Implementing it is extremely complex. Every single aspect of the firm's manufacturing operations – from machine setup to order processing, from production scheduling to personnel policy – must be fundamentally revised. Many companies are trying to introduce this approach to their own factories. Few, if any, have attained anything like Toyota's level of perfection.*

In addition, the more complex the innovation, the greater is the value to involving customers: there are simply more things to go wrong, more areas where their inputs can be of value.

These three factors should be taken into account when considering whether and to what extent customers should be involved in the innovation. As a general rule, they should be. The arguments in favour of involving customers are compelling. If management are in any doubt, then more rather than less customer involvement is a good maxim. It is only when three specific situations coincide that they should seriously consider not involving customers:

- The innovation is highly visible and will directly hurt one competitor.

- It is not a particularly radical innovation (i.e. it fits in with existing conceptual maps).

- It will be relatively easy to copy.

Otherwise, customers should always be involved as much as possible. The arguments in favour of so doing are overwhelmingly strong.

In summary, customers are a potent source of advantage in the innovative battle. Few companies make the fullest use of them. Reasons vary. In some cases they have simply not fully explored the potential ways of involving them. In other cases they overestimate the competitive risks and the value of secrecy. Whatever the reasons, most firms' innovations could benefit greatly from involving customers more. Only rarely do the potential drawbacks outweigh the benefits.

SUMMARY

Involving customers in the innovation process pays great dividends:

- Ties in with customers' own development programmes
- Builds commitment from the customer
  - to the innovation
  - more generally
- Improves quality/relevance of the innovation
- Forces the pace for management.

Few firms involve customers deeply enough

- Often for fear of increasing the competitive risks – usually misguided: competitive response is often late, rarely effective.

. . . Customers should be involved whenever possible.

7   MAKING WAY FOR INNOVATION

No product or service continues to be successful indefinitely. Eventually it declines when an innovative approach captures the market. Accepting the inevitability of change is the first stage in successful innovation. Companies must learn to challenge and discard their past successes, otherwise they become barriers to innovation.

More than this, companies should explicitly plan for the decline and withdrawal of current successes. This focuses attention on the need to innovate and makes the decline phase of the product life cycle more profitable.

7 MAKING WAY FOR INNOVATION

- The inevitability of change

- Innovators: losers as well as gainers

- Trapped by success

- Shaking off the past

THE INEVITABILITY OF CHANGE

All products, services and processes are eventually usurped. Sooner or later a better approach or technology emerges to take over the market. This phenomenon is clearest in high-technology areas, where the pace of change can be blisteringly quick (witness the speed with which 64k RAMs replaced 32k RAMs, only to be overtaken in turn by 256k RAMs). High-tech companies are familiar with the pace of change, and must live with it on a daily basis. Such changes take place in every market, however, no matter how mature or stable it may appear to be:

■ *The steel industry would perhaps be most people's archetypal idea of a mature business. Despite this it continues to develop. Blast furnace and oxygen converter technology replaced open hearth furnaces and Bessemer converters in the quest for improved efficiency. They in turn have lost ground to mini mills with electric arc technology. Continuous casting has largely taken over from previous methods. The industry never stays still for long, it continues to evolve.*

■ *Basic foodstuffs should arguably be among the most mature of all industries. Sugar is a mature commodity product. In the space of a few short years, however, it lost its largest single market worldwide: the US soft drinks industry. A cheaper substitute, high fructose corn syrup (HFCS), had emerged and rapidly captured a dominant share of this market segment. This product evolution determines company fortunes: Gulf & Western, the leader in the US sucrose industry, lost its leadership to A. E. Stanley, the largest HFCS producer.*

Saccharin has similarly been around for years. It is losing ground rapidly to a new sweetener, aspartame (or NutraSweet) which has none of saccharin's bitter after-taste. Aspartame is even making inroads into sugar's markets to an extent never achieved by saccharin. Nobody knows how far these substitutions will go, but one thing is clear: this basic commodity market is undergoing extremely rapid change.

Few markets remain stable for long. When they are stable, it usually means that some discontinuity is either just around the corner, or is already starting to happen. This is not accidental. Stable technologies and markets are symptomatic of approaches which have neared the end of their useful lives. There is limited scope for further improvement. When that situation arises businesses start to look for fundamentally different ways of tackling the problem. The discontinuity soon follows.

McKinsey developed its S-curve as a model for technology and market development* (Figure 17). The typical pattern is for things to develop very slowly at first: basic technical questions have to be resolved, customers have to be introduced to the new concept, and prices are often high initially. Once things become more established growth and progress can be extremely rapid. Soon afterwards the market approaches maturity. The concept (technological or otherwise) is close to the limits of its development: further investment and effort result in ever smaller advances. (For example, by the early 1900s commercial sailing vessels were reaching the limits of their potential. They were unable to compete with the rapidly improving performance of steamships. High-bypass turbofan jet engines may be reaching a similar stage today: further improvements in fuel efficiency may require a shift to a new technology, such as the prop-jet.)

This maturation is a warning signal. It means that there is only limited mileage left in the old way of doing things. Although the rate of progress may slow down, the competitive pressure to advance does not. Before long some fundamentally new approach will be found which has the potential to take things on to the next stage. A new S-curve begins, and the whole process repeats itself.

---

* *This is described by Richard K. Foster in* Innovation: The Attacker's Advantage *(Summit Books, 1986).*

Figure 17: The S-curve model shows how technologies and markets typically start slowly, go through a rapid growth phase and then gradually mature.

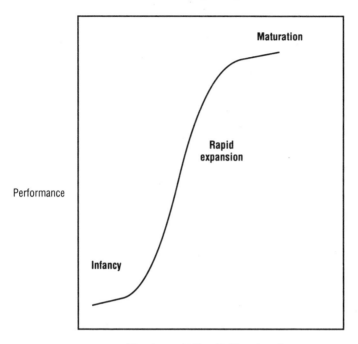

Time (or cumulative effort/investment)

INNOVATORS: LOSERS AS WELL AS GAINERS

Innovators are normally the beneficiaries of such change. In many cases they create the discontinuity itself. In others they spot the opportunities which it brings, and exploit them. Every innovation takes business away from existing companies, the incumbents in the market. Valve manufacturers lost out to transistor producers. Bias ply tyres gave way to radials. Each such transition forces the incumbent competitor to adapt to the change, or see his market share shrink inexorably. We are all used to this. The vision of the innovator changing the fundamentals of the business and stealing the market from under the noses of the established suppliers is a widespread one. What is not so often appreciated is that the innovators themselves come under pressure as the market continues to evolve. In today's competitive environment this happens increasingly rapidly:

■ *Transitron was one of the darlings of Wall Street in the late 1950s. It had a dominant position in the emerging germanium semiconductor industry, with the rapidly growing sales and profits to match. At its peak the company's stock was selling at a P/E ratio of 56 times.*

Germanium, however, was nearing the limits of its development. It was about to be replaced by silicon, a semiconducting material with the scope for even greater performance and efficiency. (Silicon has a higher band gap than germanium. It is therefore less sensitive to impurities in the manufacturing process. As a result components made from it have lower failure rates and are therefore more economical to produce and use). Wedded to its germanium technology, Transitron missed the fundamental importance of this discontinuity. The company dabbled in silicon but never gave it a high priority. It assumed that its germanium based business would continue indefinitely. Naturally, it did not. In the face of the new silicon technology, offering users improved performance and economy, the company's germanium business dwindled in size and rapidly became unprofitable. By trying to hold on to its existing business the company missed the even larger opportunities which were emerging elsewhere.

■ *The video industry in the UK has been dramatically successful. Within the space of a decade the penetration of homes with VCRs reached and passed 50 per cent. This spawned a whole new industry, the cassette rentals business. For about one-third the price of a movie ticket, VCR owners can rent a recent film to be viewed in the comfort of their own homes. It has changed the whole nature of film-going in the UK: four times as many people see recent films on video as see them in a movie theatre.*

New and potent competition is emerging, however. New broadcasting techniques – cable and direct broadcast satellites – will soon make film channels available in millions of viewers' homes. These are inherently superior technologies. They are far more cost-effective than the duplication, distribution, stocking and rental of individual cassettes, and also save the viewer from making a trip to the rental outlet. They bring films into the viewers' homes. Rental still has one advantage: the level of choice which is possible. The next few years will be interesting to watch. Will the video rentals industry adapt to the new competition and focus on its own strengths, or will it do what so many industries in similar positions have done in the past: do nothing and hope that the problem will go away?

TRAPPED BY SUCCESS

Despite all the evidence, however, many firms appear to believe that their successful products and businesses will continue to be cash cows indefinitely. They act as if the levels of profitability which they currently enjoy will continue like annuities. This has at least three undesirable consequences for how the company behaves:

- **Awareness:** if managers believe that the current business will remain secure indefinitely, they are unlikely to keep an adequate watching brief for changes in the industry. New approaches and concepts which might threaten their business can easily go unnoticed until it is too late to respond effectively.

- **The need to innovate:** the perceived need to innovate is in some senses inversely proportional to the perceived security of the existing business. If managers think that their current business will continue to earn satisfactory profits indefinitely, they are unlikely to put much effort into the search for innovation. Hunger – and a little fear – are major contributors to creativity and effort.

- **Profitabiltiy:** the eventual decline of a product can be extremely profitable – or extremely unprofitable. Which one it is depends in large part upon management actions. If the likelihood of decline is spotted early enough, managers can often take steps to milk cash out of the business as it is overtaken by the new technology. They can of course also invest in the emerging concept. Conversely, if the threat is not spotted until very late, then the firm can easily waste huge amounts of money trying to shore up an unsalvageable situation. Early warning of these fundamental changes is therefore incredibly valuable. Not having it can be very expensive.

SHAKING OFF THE PAST

The most valuable step which companies can take is to accept the inevitability of change and the transitory nature of individual successes in a changing environment. It is only by doing this that they will learn to let go of the past so that they can embrace the future. Accepting the eventual decline of current businesses is the vital first step in recognizing the need for innovation. Few leading companies do however. Richard

Foster* likens the companies which behave in this way to the mythical phoenix, the bird which repeatedly destroyed itself in order to rise again from the ashes. These firms recognise that they must ruthlessly cannibalize their current businesses just when they are at their most successful, and begin the search for a new approach, a better solution.

Many companies pay lip service to the inevitability of change and the need for innovation. At heart, however, they appear to believe that the future will be very much like the past, that the established order will continue. They focus their efforts on optimizing the efficiency of their current operations, rather than searching for new ways of delivering value. Some companies, however – ones like IBM, Hewlett-Packard, Procter & Gamble, ICL and Kwik-Fit, have taken on board the inevitability of change, and with it the need to cast aside familiar formulae for success in the search for innovation. For they know that, while innovation may be risky, it is nowhere near as dangerous as failing to adapt.

Beyond generating a widespread recognition of the inevitability of change, there are a number of specific actions which firms can and do take:

- **The outsider:** organizational inertia is a powerful barrier to change. The established and successful organization operates as a status quo machine. Often the only way to cast aside past successes is to operate outside the main body of the organization. Only outsiders have the required objectivity and freedom from emotional baggage which are needed to think the really radical thoughts:

  - *While most IBM products go through a well laid-out eight-phase development process, the PC did not. It bypassed the standard channels. A separate group was set up in Boca Raton, reporting directly to Chairman John Opel. IBM had recognized that speed and radical thinking were necessary if it was to succeed in the PC market. This was the best way to achieve them.*

  - *Du Pont, on the other hand, tried to develop polyester within its established nylon tyre cord business. The forces of the status quo proved to be too strong for the emerging technology: the nylon business saw the new material as a direct threat, and held back on its development. The*

---

* *In* Innovation: The Attacker's Advantage.

company failed to make the required commitment to the new material, and fell behind Celanese, who grabbed the lead in this developing market.

● **Making innovation explicit:** few companies explicitly measure what proportion of their sales are generated by old product lines, and what proportion come from new ones. Doing so can reinforce for managers the importance of not relying too heavily on their established sources of business.

■ *3M measures this explicitly, and gives managers targets for what proportion of sales should come from products developed in the last five years.*

● **Planning the decline:** most companies plan the launch and development of new products with great care. How many put as much effort into the decline phase of the product life cycle? Very few. Many high-tech companies have learned to operate in an environment of rapid change and short product life cycles. They accept the decline of products as an inescapable part of business life, and plan for it accordingly.

■ *One leading British computer company divides the development of its products into seven distinct phases:*
   ★ *1 Basic evaluation of the concept*
   ★ *2 Detailed feasibility and planning*
   ★ *3 First exposure to customers*
   ★ *4 Full launch onto the market*
   ★ *5 Full-scale marketing*
   ★ *6 Planning for withdrawal*
   ★ *7 Withdrawal.*

Adopting an approach such as this is an amazingly powerful tool for companies which wish to innovate. Firstly, it can help to make the final decline and withdrawal of each product far more profitable by focusing attention explicitly on it. Secondly, and even more importantly, it forces managers to change their whole approach to innovation. By accepting the transitory nature of each product's life cycle, it is no longer possible to consider individual innovations to be a final or permanent solution. Instead, they have to be considered for what they really are: one stage in a continuing flow of innovations, part of an ongoing process of developing new ways of delivering greater customer value.

The natural focus for innovators' efforts is always the new concept itself, the new venture. Innovations must, however, be viewed in the context of the firm's ongoing operations. Every innovation affects the demand for existing products or services, as customers switch to the improved solution. Accepting the inevitability of the decline of established products is a prerequisite for successful innovation. Unless firms learn to discard their past and present successes, they will never be able to develop and grow tomorrow's winners. Smoothly managing the transitions between old and new products is a skill which firms with pretensions to continuous innovation must learn to master.

SUMMARY

No product or service continues to be successful indefinitely.

- Eventually it declines when an innovative approach captures the market.

Firms must accept the eventual decline of their existing products, services and processes.

- Otherwise they become barriers to innovation.

Explicitly planning for the eventual decline and withdrawal of current products can be of major benefit.

- Focuses attention on the need for innovation.

- Removes inherent barriers to innovation.

- Makes the decline phase of the product life cycle more profitable.

8 LESS CAN BE MORE

Innovation is about new ways of delivering customer value. It need not involve additional new products or services at all. Many successful innovators create value by taking existing products or services and focusing carefully on the needs of narrowly defined segments.

This will become an increasingly important pattern for innovators. Less can be more.

8 LESS CAN BE MORE

- Additive innovation

- Focused innovation

- Defying conventional wisdom

- A strategic perspective

ADDITIVE INNOVATION

Mention innovation to most managers and they will first think of new products or services. We are conditioned to think of progress itself in terms of 'more' – more new products, more new services, more opportunities. Indeed many innovations are precisely that – additional products or services which either identify new customer needs or meet existing ones better than currently available solutions. Sony's Walkman and 3M's Post-It notepads created the demand for products which had not existed before, while EMI's CAT scanner and Smith Kline's Tagamet anti-ulcer drug met needs which had already been clearly identified but which were not adequately satisfied.

FOCUSED INNOVATION

Yet not all innovations are like this. Innovation is about finding new ways of delivering customer value, not about new products per se. It need not involve a new product or service at all – it can be some other change to the process by which value is delivered to customers. Most significantly, many innovators manage to deliver greater customer value simply by focusing on a narrower range of customers' needs: less can be more. Several fundamental trends combine to make this a particularly fruitful form of innovation:

- **The limits of scale:** in many industries the limits of economies of scale have been reached. Several competitors often have equally efficient facilities. Greater volume no longer guarantees markedly superior costs. Changes in production technology in several industries (in particular, the introduction of flexible manufacturing systems) have created new opportunities for the small and focused supplier. Their cost levels can often match, it not beat, those of their larger competitors. A high market share no longer guarantees success: it is frequently far more important to utilize assets efficiently and to target customers' needs carefully (Figure 18).

Figure 18: Scale economies are less important than previously in many industries. As a result the key factors for success have changed.

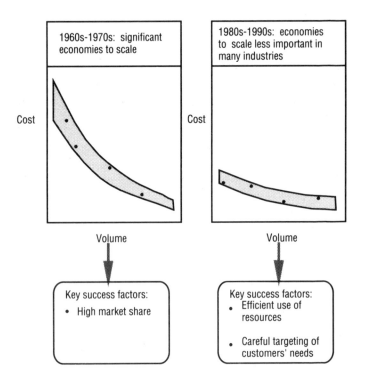

- **Diseconomies of scale:** these are becoming increasingly important in several industries. Large competitors are often at a cost disadvantage due to their very size, or, more correctly, to their diversity and spread. They suffer from the costs of complexity: diverse and complex organizations often have higher overhead levels and far less efficient communication and decision-making processes than their smaller, more focused competitors.

- **Attitudes:** attitudes towards the value of integration are changing. After decades during which it was implicitly assumed that successful companies had to provide a comprehensive range of functions in-house, companies are increasingly prepared to subcontract or purchase a whole range of products and services which they have hitherto provided for themselves. Cost effectiveness and quality are the deciding factor. This increased willingness to shop around is in itself a reflection of competitive pressures and the search for increased customer value. It creates great opportunities for efficiently focused suppliers in a whole range of industries, from cleaning services to computer software.

These trends continue to gather pace. They are altering the basic structure of many industries. They indicate that focusing on a narrow subset of customers' needs will be of increasing importance as a source of innovative opportunities. Tomorrow belongs to the specialized supplier. Countless major innovations have already resulted from this approach:

- *Kwik-Fit has changed the way in which motorists acquire replacement exhausts and tyres for their cars: 60 per cent of the market is now via fitting centres. It will increasingly be the same for brakes, steering, clutches and other major components. This business is founded upon one simple premise: that the traditional full-service repair garage is fundamentally less efficient than a high-volume outlet focused on a narrow range of products and services.*

- *House conveyancing in the UK is still largely the preserve of broadly-based firms of solicitors. Their operations are set up to provide the full range of legal services, private as well as commercial in most cases. This breadth of competence is reflected in their cost structure and scale of fees. Many house purchases are relatively simple: the conveyancing can be done by firms which focus exclusively on this function. With a more mechanized approach to their business and a less highly qualified (i.e. less expensive) mix of staff, they can price extremely competitively. They are likely to gain significant market share from traditional solicitors in this specialized field in future.*

■ *Similar things have already happened to several aspects of the medical care industry in the US. Specialized narrow-range operators have proved to be extremely cost effective in several areas. Others will follow. What of maternity care? In most cases it need not be provided in a full hospital (i.e. expensive) environment. Specialized 'maternity motels' would be far more efficient, particularly if located adjacent to hospitals so that help is near in case of emergency.*

■ *Bank One grew extremely rapidly and profitably in the 1970s and 1980s by adopting a focused strategy. It honed its transaction processing skills and efficiency and offered these as a back-office service to other banks. It has client banks in every state of the US and is now one of the country's leading regional banks.*

■ *After a decade during which the conventional wisdom in financial circles has been that banks will have to provide a complete range of services in order to be successful, those perceptions are changing. Bankers are realizing that for most banks the best route to success will be to concentrate on a few core areas of strength. Identifying innovative ways of segmenting customers' needs to provide carefully focused product and service packages will be a successful strategy for an increasing number of players in this rapidly evolving industry. (The Big Bang in the UK is a particular example of how opportunities have been created for narrow-range specialized suppliers. In the business market a number of corporate finance boutiques have been set up, each supplying a carefully defined range of services. In the personal market companies like the Mortgage Corporation have prospered by offering one single product.)*

DEFYING CONVENTIONAL WISDOM

The conventional wisdom in consumer goods has always been that more products are a good thing. Line extensions and variants have been used to exploit the strengths of successful existing brands. In many cases this is worthwhile. In others, however, it merely contributes to a proliferating portfolio of individually small products. This not only adds to complexity and overheads but can also blunt the firm's marketing efforts as attention and resources are spread between too many conflicting priorities. Moreover, developments in the retail trade are reducing the potential value of such a broad product range. On the one hand, retailers are becoming increasingly sophisticated. Access to greater information is enabling them to weed out the more marginal products: supermarket shelf space will increasingly be made available only to those products which have a real and valid role to play. On the other hand a number of developments (such as centralized distribution) mean that the economics no longer favour a broad product range to the same extent as before.

- *Some astute companies have already spotted and exploited these trends. Others will follow. United Biscuits undertook a wholesale review of its product range, weeding out several marginal performers. The overall result was a significant improvement to several aspects of the business, from manufacturing all the way through to brand management.*

Examples of focused innovation exist in many industries. The details may differ, but the central theme is the same: delivering greater value by specializing. Firms can focus in two ways: either by supplying some narrow subset of customers' needs or by supplying the needs of a tightly defined group of customers. Both approaches can be successful.

A STRATEGIC PERSPECTIVE

The historic pattern in many industries has been one of broad-range suppliers. The approach of the leading competitors reflects this: they commonly supply a wide range of products to a diverse group of customers. Their past success frequently reinforces this view. Their own innovative efforts are most naturally directed at providing more, not less. Their biggest blind spot is to the focused competitor who innovates in some carefully identified customer, product or service niche. This creates the opportunity for the young or start-up company. It can often slip by unnoticed for long enough to establish a strong defensible position in its niche: by the time the market leader responds it is often too late for him to do anything.

Creating value through careful focus will be increasingly important across a diverse spread of industries. The opportunity for innovators has seldom been greater. What is required above all is a radical approach, a fresh look at how it is that value is delivered to customers. What are they really buying? Which products and services are currently bundled together? Why? Which could be spun off and provided in a different way? Would doing so result in cost savings or better value? Would customers be prepared to buy what they need in this way?

SUMMARY

Innovation is about new ways of delivering customer value.

- It need not involve new products or services.

In many industries focusing on a narrow range of customer's needs can result in major cost savings compared with broad-line suppliers.

- This will be an increasingly important source of innovative opportunities – less can be more.

9 ORGANIZING FOR INNOVATION

There is no one organization type uniquely best suited to innovation. Different structures work well for different companies.

Although there is no one right answer, there are several wrong ones. Some structures severely inhibit innovation: they act as barriers to change. Companies should be organized to break down these barriers.

9 ORGANIZING FOR INNOVATION

- Success through a range of styles

- The organizational objectives
  - Integrating inputs
  - Exploiting specialization
  - Breaking down the barriers
  - Structure following strategy
  - Innovations and innovativeness
  - Team dynamics

- Resolving the conflicts

SUCCESS THROUGH A RANGE OF STYLES

What type of organization structure is most appropriate for innovative firms? Are some structures more effective than others in helping companies to be innovative? The empirical evidence is, on the face of it, far from conclusive. Firms with a wide variety of styles and structures can be successful innovators:

- *Toyota's Production System is an ongoing process of innovation which is integrated into the day-to-day running of the whole firm. It affects every aspect of the company's operations. All employees are solicited for their suggestions for improvements to the process. They contribute over two million per year, 96 per cent of which are implemented. The entire company is involved.*

- *IBM's PC has been a truly major success for the company. It was developed by an independent group of managers working well away from the influence of the main body of the organization. This project was a high corporate priority, reporting directly to Chairman John Opel. Several other companies have used such 'skunk works' in similar situations with success.*

- *3M is a consistently innovative launcher of new products. It has a strong culture of innovation. Managers are allowed to pursue their own pet projects with minimal interference from the company, provided they meet their other business responsibilities. 'Bootlegging' is an accepted corporate practice. As a result several projects are underway at any one time, many of which the company has little control over. Some of 3M's most successful new businesses have arisen in this way.*

- *After its initial success Federal Express set up a sort of corporate innovation centre. It is run by a small group of some of the company's founding employees. Their only responsibility is to consider new opportunities for the company, wherever they may lie. It looks both at ways of improving Federal's base business and also at unrelated diversifications. It has evaluated and rejected dirigibles as a means of saving fuel. It evaluated and accepted installation of computer terminals in all the company's trucks.*

- *Kwik-Fit is continually testing new variations on its original rapid service theme. The responsibility for generating and evaluating new ideas is assumed by Tom Farmer and a small group of the firm's founding managers. They have frequent strategy sessions at which they consider and debate possible new approaches. This is done alongside their other full-time responsibilities.*

THE ORGANIZATIONAL OBJECTIVES

There are clearly no black and white answers. The approach which works for one firm would be entirely inappropriate for many others. The organization structure must be tailored to suit the firm's people, environment and culture. There has to be a coherence or fit between them. Although there are no hard and fast rules, there are a number of guidelines which managers should consider before settling upon the right structure to suit their particular needs. Equally important, while there is no structure which can guarantee success, there are a number of organization types which tend to hinder innovative activity. Avoiding these pitfalls is important in itself: doing so can markedly shorten the odds on success. The right structure must satisfy a number of (partly conflicting) objectives.

Integrating inputs

Strategic innovation is inherently integrative in nature. It is about finding new ways of delivering value to customers. Creating that new value can come from making changes to any aspect of the firm's operations. Increasingly frequently it comes from the way in which the various parts combine to make up the whole (i.e. business system innovation). There has to be a common purpose between the different parts of the business.

Successful innovation therefore requires integrating inputs from all key functions and disciplines within the business. Focusing attention on individual aspects in isolation may optimize the firm's performance in each area, but is unlikely to result in true strategic innovation. Worse still, separately optimizing individual aspects of the business may actually detract value from the total customer offering: the most cost effective manufacturing policy may reduce the firm's responsiveness to customers' needs, the widest product range may have unacceptable cost implications, and so on.

Exploiting specialization

Innovation may require integrating inputs, but efficiency calls for specialization. Ever since Adam Smith (and before), operations within businesses have become increasingly specialized in the quest for greater efficiency. To discard specialization in the name of promoting integration across functions would be folly. There is a natural conflict here. The firm has to reach a compromise between its needs for efficiency and innovation.

Breaking down the barriers

All organizations have in-built barriers to innovation. The more successful the firm is the stronger these barriers tend to be. Established structures and cultures act as a status quo machine, preserving the current equilibrium and inhibiting change. True innovation is iconoclastic. It requires that accepted truths are questioned and that established ideas are turned on their heads. Few organizations do this of their own accord. Change has to be forced upon the organization. The forces of inertia and vested interests have to be broken down or sidestepped.

Companies have several ways of doing this. One was discussed earlier: to establish a completely independent unit to pursue the innovation, as in IBM's PC. Another approach is to organize the firm so as to minimize the adverse effects of inertia and vested interests. This is effectively what Procter & Gamble did many years ago when it invented the concept of the product manager. In this system individuals are fully responsible for the success of their own products. Most importantly, they are free to adopt their own strategy, even where this entails competing with other products belonging to the parent company. The whole system is structured to minimize the constraints encumbering the individual product and manager.

Structure following strategy

Firms which organize themselves along the lines of strategic business units (SBUs) are making similar assumptions, and should be able to maximize their responsiveness to the strategic needs of each business. This is indeed a valuable directional step. The big potential problem is that the boundaries between SBUs change over time. In particular, innovations can change the most logical definition of the SBU. What was one SBU yesterday can easily be two or three today or vice versa. The structure which worked well before can rapidly become a major impediment to innovation. None of this detracts from the fundamental benefits of SBU organization. What it does imply is that the most appropriate organization structure changes with time. The most innovative firms will sometimes appear to be organizational chameleons, forever adapting to new needs as they emerge.

Innovations and innovativeness

There is a distinction between innovations and innovativeness. Some innovations can be considered as stand-alone entities in isolation from the rest of the business. (Many straightforward product or service innovations fall into this category.) It can be appropriate to consider such innovations in an organizationally independent manner. It is precisely for this type of innovation that many companies have successfully used independent 'skunk works': the value of independence far outweighs the benefits of integration with the rest of the organization. Most pharmaceutical companies organize their R&D departments in this way. (Incidentally, this example demonstrates the need for organizations to change as the innovative environment evolves. Isolated and independent R&D centres worked well when the key to success in the pharmaceutical industry was to discover major breakthrough drugs. The industry has changed: it is equally important today fully to exploit existing drugs by developing line extensions and formulations targeted at the needs of specific segments. This calls for much closer coordination between R&D and the marketing and sales functions. Sadly, relatively few pharmaceutical companies have made these changes.)

Innovativeness, however, is more than just a sequence of innovations. It is a fundamental aspect of a company's behaviour patterns. The most pressing need which many firms face is to become more innovative in all that they do. This type of innovation simply has to be integrated into the fabric of the organization. It cannot be tacked on or left to one side. Independent units are no solution. In fact, they can lure managers into a false sense of security: they think their organization is becoming more innovative when in fact all they are doing is pursuing isolated innovations. This type of innovation is generally far more difficult to achieve. It is a true measure of Toyota's achievement in developing its Production System.

Team dynamics

Integrating a wide range of inputs usually calls for a team effort. The more diverse the inputs needed are, the larger the team is required to be. There is a clear conflict here: large teams tend to be less effective in many respects than smaller ones. If the goal of the team is to work effectively together and to be truly creative, then five or six members seems to be as large as it can go. Any larger and it risks becoming a committee.

The constraints of team dynamics need to be considered alongside what might be termed the 'centre of gravity' of the innovative effort. In some firms the type of innovation sought is such that it is relatively senior managers who are best positioned to provide the inputs which are needed. If this is the case, it argues strongly for one or two small teams drawn from top management. In other situations, however, it is the more junior managers and workers who have most to contribute. (This is the case for Toyota as it continues developing its production system.) In these situations a much larger number of teams is more appropriate, each composed of more junior staff.

RESOLVING THE CONFLICTS

The organization is the medium through which a firm's management achieves results. Choosing the best structure is one of the most powerful tools which they have at their disposal in the search for innovation. There are no universally right or wrong answers. The organization which satisfies one goal will fail on another. A compromise must be reached between conflicting sets of goals. The most appropriate solution depends upon the specifics of each individual situation. Frequently this solution may be impractical for any number of reasons. In the real world this kind of problem is inevitable. What is clear is that the organization structure chosen profoundly influences the firm's innovative performance. No structure should be adopted without considering its likely effect on this increasingly important aspect of the firm's performance.

SUMMARY

There is no uniquely best organization structure from an innovation point of view:

- Different structures work well for different companies
- Important to tailor the structure to the firm's specific situation.

There are a number of guidelines which innovative firms should bear in mind:

- Organize to integrate inputs from several disciplines
  - break down functional barriers.
- Distinguish between innovations and innovativeness:
  - independent teams vs integrating into the organization.
- Break down barriers to innovation:
  - independent teams
  - product managers, SBUs.
- Utilize team dynamics:
  - maximum effective size is five or six members.

III INNOVATION AND THE FIRM

10 INNOVATION AND THE MATURE COMPANY

Mature firms have inherent strengths and weaknesses in the search for innovation. These effect every stage of the process, from accepting the need for innovation to its implementation.

Mature firms are rarely as innovative as they should be. Their biggest failing is that they approach innovative ventures as if they themselves were mature businesses. They are not. Changing this approach can transform their performance.

10 INNOVATION AND THE MATURE COMPANY

- Perpetuating success

- The mature firm's strengths

- Barriers to innovation
  - Perceiving the need for innovation
  - Generating the ideas
  - Evaluating the opportunity
  - Implementing innovation

- The vicious circle

- Breaking the vicious circle and reasserting control

- Building on strength
  - Market knowledge
  - Contacts and credibility
  - Testing the water

- Removing the barriers
  - Perceiving the need for innovation
  - Generating the ideas
  - Evaluating the opportunity
  - Implementing innovation
  - Changing the culture

PERPETUATING SUCCESS

Innovation is the greatest challenge facing businesses today. Nowhere is this more true than in the successful mature company. It has progressed from birth through the growth and consolidation phases of its development. It has adapted effectively to the particular demands of each phase. Its overall behaviour patterns have evolved as it has grown. Originally highly adaptive, they are now likely to be more repetitive, for success in the mature business demands strong repetitive skills: building efficiency, careful attention to detail and continuous optimization within the existing business framework. It is now at a watershed. To focus exclusively on perfecting its base business may yield steady profits in the short term – but in the long term can lead only to stagnation and eventual decline. No product or service can continue to be fine-tuned indefinitely. Sooner or later some discontinuity will fundamentally alter the market. It could come from any quarter – technological change, new customer needs, new distribution channels or whatever. Only one thing is certain: it will come. Failure to innovate is a guarantee of eventual decline. Yet innovation itself is risky, and often runs counter to every instinct of the mature firm.

The real challenge is to adapt once more. By striving for and achieving a balance between its repetitive skills and the adaptive skills of the young growth firm (see Chapter 14, Adaptive and Repetitive Behaviour) it can replicate and extend its early success. It can become continuously innovative, with a steady stream of new ventures under development. At any time it will have a number of businesses, each at a different stage of the cycle (Figure 19). The management skills required differ markedly. Balance is required. Achieving this balance is not easy. The firm must foster and accommodate fundamentally different behavioural styles within the one organization. This creates tensions. Managing these tensions is the key organizational skill which is required.

Figure 19: Continuous innovation can give the mature company secure and steady growth.

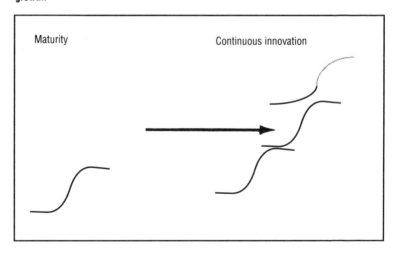

THE MATURE FIRM'S STRENGTHS

The search for innovation is an integral part of the ongoing competitive battle. The mature company has a number of advantages over the start-up firm:

- **The baseload:** the mature firm has a baseload of business which can support new ventures. This is a great advantage. A single innovation can make or break the new firm; this is seldom the case for the mature company. It can not only afford to keep faith and stick with the new venture when it runs into problems (and most will), but can also experiment with more new ideas and variations to the concept. It simply has more time and resources with which to get the concept right.

- **Market knowledge:** this should be an invaluable asset. Years of hard-won experience give it a resource which few start-up firms can match. It probably has an extensive database of market research. Properly managed, this information can be a rich source of innovative ideas.

- **Contacts and credibility:** these are among the most significant advantages which the established firm can have in many markets. This applies not only to customers but also to suppliers, distribution channels, potential recruits and so on. Often, trying out a new product or service entails significant risks for the customer. Life can be extremely difficult for the new entrant in such markets. The customer's cost of switching is simply too high to take risks with a new supplier. It is often far easier for the established and trusted supplier to start the dialogue that will lead to customers trying out a new product:

  ■ *A new entrant tried for several years to introduce a fundamentally new concept to the small horsepower electric motor business. It failed. In part this was due to the conservatism of the major original equipment manufacturer (OEM) customers. For them the risks (business as well as technical) of engineering the new motor into their products were simply too great. How different might the end result have been if one of the industry's established suppliers had introduced the new motor?*

- **Testing the water:** often the viability of a new concept rests upon two or three critical assumptions. In many cases it is not known at the outset whether they are valid or not. They have to be tested. The start-up company must often proceed a long way down the track with its innovation to test fully these assumptions. This usually takes time and entails committing most of the company's resources. It is highly risky. The mature firm on the other hand can often test new ideas on a marginal basis: it can switch a small number of outlets over to a new business format for a trial period, or test the key aspects of change to a product or process on a sample of customers or on one of its production lines. By so doing it can save both time and money, testing the concept without committing the same level of resources. It can therefore reduce the risks inherent in innovating.

BARRIERS TO INNOVATION

So far, so good. Mature companies have many inherent strengths in the search for innovation. Yet most mature companies are not as innovative as they should be. Why not? Opposing the above theoretical advantages are a number of barriers. These barriers occur in all stages of the innovation process (Figure 20). They stop the mature firm from being as innovative as it could and should be.

Figure 20: Mature firms face barriers to innovation in all phases of the innovative process.

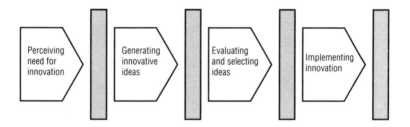

Perceiving the need for innovation

There is an increased general awareness of the need to become more innovative. But that awareness is only rarely translated into action. There are still many mature firms which do not place a sufficiently high priority on developing new ideas and ventures. They continue to act as if a narrow focus on efficiency within an established framework will guarantee success for the long term. Often, the need to adapt and evolve is not fully appreciated until a competitor has stolen the lead with some new concept. By then it may be too late. There are a number of reasons why mature firms tend to behave in this way:

- **The myth of the mature market:** there is often a feeling that because the firm and the industry are currently mature and stable, they will continue to be so forever. Therefore, this line of reasoning goes on, innovation is neither appropriate nor important in this industry: we can continue to operate within well established frameworks. Optimizing our current operations has a far greater payoff than searching for new ideas in what by now is a well-ploughed furrow.

  ■ *Belief in the maturity of markets is not new. There was actually a proposal in 1905 to close the US Patent Office, on the grounds that there were no inventions left to be made!*

- **The weight of numbers:** when compared to the established business, the new venture always looks tiny, or even insignificant. It is frequently the case that some relatively small performance improvement in the firm's base business – a per cent or two off costs, a per cent or two increase in price realization – will swamp the potential contribution of the new venture over even a three- or five-year planning period. The planning director of a major retailer recognizes this problem:

  ■ *'We never give innovation the attention it warrants. There always seems to be a more pressing problem: the need to improve sales per square foot in marginal stores, to add new stores to the portfolio etc. The payoff from these moves always seems to be greater and more secure than pursuing some fundamentally new idea.'*

  With management's attention focused so strongly on the day-to-day performance of the business, innovation takes a back seat. The firm becomes trapped, continuously making marginal improvements to its performance, but never breaking out into completely new pastures. The tyranny of the status quo has set in.

- **Cannibalization:** firms sometimes actually shy away from innovating because it will cannibalize some of their existing business. They correctly identify that the new, improved idea will gain a large part of its sales volume from existing product lines – which are generating profits, employing people and in which the firm may have sunk a substantial investment. They then incorrectly assume that if *they* ignore the innovative opportunity that it will somehow go away.

● **Defining the business:** successful innovation requires taking a broad, holistic view of customers' needs. The proper focus is: what do they really want, and how can we create value for them? In contrast, many mature firms adopt a narrow perspective: how can we do better that which we are doing already? Efficiency rather than effectiveness becomes the goal. This approach can make managers and firms blind to the opportunities to restructure fundamentally the way in which they supply customers' needs.

■ *Most ocean shipping companies in the 1960s saw their role as transporting shiploads of goods on the high seas. The focus of their attention was the ship itself: how to make it larger, faster, more economic to run. The fact that burgeoning world trade was leading to hopelessly congested ports – and tying up those marvellously efficient ships and the customers' goods for days and even weeks – was unfortunate but out of their control. They did not consider it to be their problem. Sea Land did, however. It defined its role as being the transportation of customers' goods from their original source to their final destination. This led them to develop the containerization concept, offering major economies and time savings on the land and port legs of the journey. The container would be packed at the sender's premises and not unpacked until it reached its final destination. Instead of loading the ship with what could be literally thousands of odd-shaped and assorted packages, the standard-sized containers would slot into fixed racks in the hold. Time in port could be reduced to a matter of hours. The total time and cost for the customer was reduced. The rest is history. Containerization grew extremely rapidly and is now the norm for an incredibly wide range of cargoes.*

■ *A senior publishing executive described his previous employer's perspective: 'They looked upon publishing as the commissioning, printing and distribution of books: they dealt with the printed word. So when I tried to interest them in other aspects of commissioning and disseminating information – via video and audio cassettes – they were simply not interested. This form of publishing did not fit with their view of their business.'*

Many mature companies are encumbered by one or more of these problems. Although lip service may be paid to the need for investigating new ways of addressing the market, it does not progress beyond there.

The cultural fabric of the organization effectively rejects innovation as a concept. With such a low priority ascribed to developing new ideas, the company literally does not get off first base. It will never be innovative.

Generating the ideas

Innovation is inherently risky. A high proportion of new ventures will fail. To ensure success in its innovative attempts the mature firm needs a steady flow of ideas. New ideas and concepts are the raw materials from which new business opportunities are built. The isolated flash of brilliance does sometimes work. The odds, however, are against it. The mature firm needs a constant stream of ideas. For this to happen, innovation must become an integral part of the way in which the whole organization functions. It cannot remain as the exception, the isolated event. Just as in the case of accepting the basic need for innovation, however, a number of factors tend to limit the flow of new ideas in mature firms:

- **People:** a particular type of individual is attracted to the large mature organization. They tend to value what it offers: security, prestige, often the intellectual challenge of working in a sophisticated environment. They are not in general the most entrepreneurial or innovative individuals, but have skills in other areas. Their experience within the mature firm will tend to reinforce these tendencies. Clearly, there are exceptions. In particular, 'big company' people do sometimes change to become less risk averse and more entrepreneurial later in their careers. Sometimes there is an innovator waiting to break out (of this, more later). The facts are inescapable, however: managers in mature firms are unlikely to be innovators at heart.

- **Culture:** the very lifeblood of the successful mature firm is efficiency and attention to detail. These attributes maintain and reinforce the success of the company in its market. Tolerance of failure can often be very low. Experience and analysis can often remove a lot of the risk from the business. Mistakes are very expensive. There are few excuses for failure.

  Innovative new ventures are different. Risks are high. Even given the best analysis and full backing, many will fail. This sits uneasily with the culture of the mature firm. Failure is not acceptable in the company's base business, and the same attitudes spill over into new ventures. Now, shortening the odds on success is absolutely critical –

it is what accomplished and consistent innovators always do. Taking it to the next stage – a fear of failure – is disastrous. It can kill off all new ideas.

In this environment, experimenting and learning become impossible. The clearest manifestation of this often lies in the company's promotion policies and career development generally. The surest way ahead for a manager is to perform well in an important function within the core business. To be associated with a successful innovation may be of some marginal benefit to the manager, but is unlikely to make a huge difference. To be involved with a failure, however, can mean the end of an otherwise promising career. Failure in an innovative venture is often measured with the same yardstick as failure in the mature core business. The stigma attached to an unsuccessful venture is sometimes attached not only to the managers directly running it but also to those senior managers who approved and supported it in the first place. The results are obvious: innovative ideas are discouraged and, if they are put forward, are often unlikely to be approved.

The comments of a senior venture capital executive throw a stark light on this problem:

- *'Even as a partner in a venture capital firm, there is a tendency to avoid risky ventures. Although we have all had failures and cannot point the finger, one hates to be associated with a flop. Advancement in the firm is strongly influenced by the success of one's portfolio of investments: one can't afford to have too many failures. That is one reason why so much venture capital is funnelled into leveraged buyouts and the like. True seed capital is extremely risky.'*

If a well-known venture capital company can be described in this way, imagine how much more extreme is the case of the typical successful mature firm. Innovation is actively discouraged by the corporate culture. The flow of ideas has been turned off.

- **Organization structure:** The complexity of many large organizations leads to clear functional specialization and division. In a stable environment, that is often the best way to ensure efficiency in each of the individual components in the business system or value chain. This efficiency has its price, however. Innovation requires the identification of new ways of delivering customer value. It is relatively unusual for this new value to result from a change to just one link in the value chain. More usually, changes are needed in several areas simultaneously and in the way in which the different areas relate to each other or fit together. This calls for an integrated view of the business. If line managers are all functional specialists, then the only level at which this integration can take place is at the most senior echelons of management. These managers are frequently too far removed from the business to be able to provide meaningful inputs. They are simply too senior.

Thus organization structure itself can present barriers to innovation. A functionally focused structure can improve efficiency in each area of the business, but can reduce the innovative effectiveness of the whole. It can impair individual managers' ability to develop innovative ideas, even if they are keen to do so.

Taken together the above factors can severely limit the firm's ability to come up with a steady flow of – or indeed any – innovative ideas. Even assuming a recognition of the need to innovate, managers are poorly equipped to do so. Their basic skills together with the culture and structure of their company are seldom conducive to innovation. They lack the broad perspective and the risk-taking, frame-breaking approach which underlies all truly successful and strategic innovations.

Evaluating the opportunity

The investment appraisal methods used in mature firms tend to rely heavily on financial analysis (see Chapter 5, Evaluating the Opportunity). These methods work quite well for low risk investments in mature parts of the business: capacity additions, cost reduction investments etc. They work less well for speculative ventures. They simply require too much data while at the same time eliciting insufficient information that is truly valuable:

- Unrealistically precise levels of financial data are needed to form the basis for detailed projections and evaluations.

- The really critical strategic assumptions underlying the innovation are often ignored. Managers are so pressed to collect and analyse the financial data required that they have little time to ask the fundamental questions which will determine the venture's success or failure. For precisely whom will we create value? How? What do they do today? In what way is our idea different, and why is it better? And so on.

The result is an evaluation process with two critical weaknesses:

- **Bias:** it is biased against truly innovative (and hence risky) ventures and towards safer ones. The majority of investments approved tend to be those offering marginal performance improvements to the core business of the firm, rather than significantly new ventures. The need for hard quantitative data favours the former at the expense of the latter. The process is driving the strategy, rather than the other way around.

- **Efficiency:** it is an inefficient screen for innovative ventures. The likelihood of any being approved is quite low, but the method fails to distinguish the real winners from the also-rans. It simply does not ask the right strategic questions.

As a backlash against such financially orientated approaches, some firms have moved towards looser evaluation methods for their corporate venturing programmes. Generally the results are disappointing. The most common result tends to be the approval of a greater proportion of investment proposals, but no improvement in the ability to distinguish between winners and losers. Clearly, improvement is needed in how mature firms evaluate and choose between proposals for new ventures.

Implementing innovation

Assuming that the proposal has been accepted, the new venture has to be launched. It must be transferred from being a concept and a plan into a real business. While large firms have many advantages here (which were alluded to earlier) they are also beset by disadvantages:

- **People:** as noted earlier, large and mature firms are simply not the best place to go looking for entrepreneurs. The people they attract in the first place and subsequently nurture are seldom those needed for building a new business. Clearly there are exceptions – if there were not, the situation would be extremely dire. The mature firm has to seek out and exploit these exceptions. Even when the budding entrepreneur has been found or come forward, however, problems remain: the skills and attitudes needed to build a new venture are very different to those needed to succeed in an established firm (see Chapter 14, Adaptive and Repetitive Behaviour). Admittedly, the mature executive who decides to pursue an innovative opportunity within his company has a lot of experience which will be of immense value to him. However, he also has a lot of experience which will be positively disadvantageous. Many of the hard-won and engrained lessons will be simply inappropriate to running a young and growing firm. Unlearning has to take place.

- **Resources and cost structures:** there can sometimes be a tendency to smother the new venture with resources. Let's assume that it has been identified as a really attractive opportunity and therefore a high priority for the firm. Senior management will then sometimes actually commit too many resources to the new venture. There is sometimes even an implicit assumption that money can solve all problems which will arise along the way. In reality the reverse is true: having too many resources promotes certain counter-productive attitudes within the new venture. It can lose its hard cutting edge. Often neither senior management nor the managers running the new venture will realize that this is happening. Mature firms and start-ups simply do things in different ways. The best start-ups always seem to be more tight-fisted and hungry than new ventures set up by larger firms. As long as the new venture continues to be funded by its parent company, this need not matter too much. Sooner or later, however, it will have to be self-supporting. If it then finds itself competing with independent start-ups, the problems begin. It can find itself at a disadvantage due to its higher cost structure and less aggressive attitude. This applies in all types of businesses – not just those where costs are the most important competitive variable.

  ■ *A close acquaintance who recently set up a professional services company confides: 'One adopts a completely different attitude to that of one's larger competitors. We searched for six months to find the right office and a good deal – which we did, at well below the market rate. We bought flat-pack desks and assembled them over a weekend. Our fax machine is second-hand. We hire more secretarial support only when we really need it, not before.'*

  'It works. A competitor was set up at much the same time by a major financial services group. They had at least twice the capitalization we had. Not surprisingly, they've spent about twice as much as we have – without any real benefit.'

This extends beyond costs into the whole attitude with which the business is run. Entrepreneurs are always looking for the edge in what they do – they have a kind of 'killer instinct' in the way they do business. To paraphrase Dr Johnson, nothing focuses a man's mind so much as the knowledge that it is his own money which he is spending. Eddy Shah put it very succinctly: 'Necessity is the mother of innovation.'

- **The web of constraints:** new ventures within large firms frequently run foul of a whole range of corporate rules and constraints. Components cannot be purchased from such and such a supplier. Legal advice has to come from the firm's existing solicitors, who have a diverse range of company interests to protect. Staff have to be recruited to fit into existing structures and grades. The new venture cannot compete with other divisions of the firm. And so on. Some will not matter very much, others will be rather important. Taken together, however, they form a cocoon of regulations that the new business may never break out of. Innovation is difficult enough as it is. Doing it with one hand tied behind one's back is nigh-on impossible. Needless to say, the independent start-up has none of these concerns. Often the real difference is not the individual constraints per se, but their knock-on effect: they divert management time and effort from the real work of building the business and winning customers. They are a hidden cost which the large firm's new venture must bear.

- **Decision-making:** mature firms usually operate with carefully developed decision-making processes. These have value – they provide coherence, stability and control over the actions which individual managers take. They prevent rash and ill-considered actions from being taken. They provide the mature firm with a much-needed safety valve. They also slow things down. For the new venture this is unacceptable. It simply cannot work with a slow-moving decision-making process. Sometimes quite fundamental changes of direction are needed, modifying the innovative concept in the light of experience. If this requires approval from the parent company, then meetings have to be convened. Further information is asked for and debated and decisions (usually compromises) are reached. In that time the independent start-up could well have tried out the changes and moved on to something else again. The downside for the subsidiary of the mature firm is two-fold: firstly the time which elapses before a decision is reached, and secondly the level of management time and effort which is taken up in the process.

THE VICIOUS CIRCLE

Thus far we have been discussing each aspect of the innovation process in isolation. Clearly they interact with each other. If few proposals are being put forward for approval, then that influences how they will be evaluated. If they are evaluated in a particular way, then that influences how they will be put forward for approval. And so on. The mature firm can very easily fall into a vicious circle where it takes inappropriate actions in individual stages of the process in an attempt to meet overall innovative objectives (Figure 21).

Figure 21: Mature companies can fall into a vicious circle which inhibits innovative success.

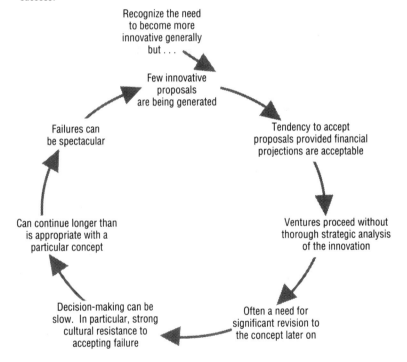

Recognize the need to become more innovative generally but . . .

Few innovative proposals are being generated

Tendency to accept proposals provided financial projections are acceptable

Ventures proceed without thorough strategic analysis of the innovation

Often a need for significant revision to the concept later on

Decision-making can be slow. In particular, strong cultural resistance to accepting failure

Can continue longer than is appropriate with a particular concept

Failures can be spectacular

In an attempt to become more innovative, the firm accepts and pursues some ventures from the limited choice of proposals being put forward. These are often proceeded upon without a thorough strategic analysis of their viability. Inevitably, problems occur. There needs to be significant revision to one or more aspects of the innovation. Then two separate weaknesses beset the firm. Firstly, there is a reluctance to accept failure: it runs against every instinct of the company and all its past experience. If a venture fails its managers are considered to have failed. So they soldier on, not acknowledging the seriousness of the situation. Secondly, by the time they recognize the need to change, deciding which way to go takes far longer than it should. All this time the clock is ticking away. Money is being spent to shore up the venture. The failure, when it comes, can be spectacular. The whole unfortunate affair is painful, scarring both the company and the individuals involved. They are left knowing that innovation is needed, but perceiving it to be extremely costly and risky. The flow of innovative ideas dries up.

BREAKING THE VICIOUS CIRCLE AND REASSERTING CONTROL

This paints a very dark picture. Taken together these inherent disadvantages that the mature company faces in innovating sound formidable. One almost wonders how such firms ever innovate successfully. Yet they do. The true situation is, of course, that they have advantages as well as disadvantages. Figure 22 lays out in one table all the positive and negative factors described above. This analysis is a powerful prescriptive tool for helping such firms become more innovative. Broadly speaking, there are two generic actions which can be taken:

- Accentuate the firm's positive aspects, **building upon strength;**

- Act in a way which counteracts or at least **minimizes the weaknesses** which mature firms so frequently have.

These actions encompass a wide variety of types. Some are individual, specific actions which can be implemented reasonably rapidly. Others relate to more diffuse aspects of the firm's organization and culture. They require sustained effort to yield results. Together they can change the firm's entire stance and performance in innovation and indeed on a broader front. They are tried and tested methods, being a formalization and systematization of what the most innovative firms already do. They provide a checklist and a framework for mature firms to follow.

Figure 22: Advantages and disadvantages which mature firms typically face in attempting to innovate.

Advantages	Disadvantages
Baseload of business • Able to support new ventures **Knowledge of the market** • Valuable source of innovative ideas • Avoiding obvious errors **Contacts and credibility** • Facilitates launching new ventures **Testing new concepts** • Able to do this on a marginal basis	**Perceiving the need for innovation** • Belief that they operate in a mature market • Focus on short-term operating improvements • Perceive innovation as cannibalizing existing business • Narrow definition of the market and the firm's role **Generating innovative ideas** • People: not typically entrepreneurs • Culture: fear of failure • Organization structure: tight functional responsibilities • Narrow definition of the business hampers the broad perspective needed for innovation **Evaluating innovative ideas** • Often over-emphasis of financial aspects at expense of a more strategic view **Implementing innovative ideas** • People do not have all of the necessary skills or attitudes • New ventures are sometimes over-resourced, which can hamper their competitiveness • Have to work within the constraints (formal and informal) of the parent organization • Decision-making tends to be structured and slow • Reluctance to admit failure and abandon the project at an appropriate time

BUILDING ON STRENGTH

Of the four factors which comprise strengths for the mature company, the first is a given: the firm either has a steady baseload of business or it does not. It need not occupy us further here. The other three factors are, however, amenable to positive action and reinforcement.

Market knowledge

This may seem such a clear advantage as to hardly warrant further consideration. To believe that , however, would be a mistake. There are two fundamentally important points which should never be lost sight of:

- **Challenge the map:** knowledge and experience can only too easily become impediments rather than strengths. The firm's history and observation of events lead it to develop a conceptual map of the way in which the market works. This process is as inevitable as it is necessary. Without some such structure, experience and information become a mere jumble of assorted facts. Learning becomes impossible, and with it managing also. A strong conceptual map is a major asset. If it is too strong, however, it starts to become counterproductive. If the framework becomes too engrained, then new information ceases to be of value. It is simply slotted into the conceptual map. If it does not fit the map, then it tends to be ignored or explained away. Conceptual maps have a valid role as filters of information, separating the valuable from the insignificant. If they are allowed to become too powerful they lose their worth, blocking the flow of all new information (see Chapter 13, Innovation and Conceptual Maps).

    This situation is frighteningly easy to fall into. Mature firms often surround themselves with a wealth of quantitative data on their market and their business. These numbers provide a high degree of comfort and a feeling of security: everything is under control, we know everything there is to know about our market. Meanwhile, the numbers can actually disguise the reality and divert management's attention from fundamental changes which have taken place in the environment. The numbers and the map take the place of reality.

    ▪ *A well-known maker of ultrasonic testing equipment had dominated the offshore testing market for many years. Its products were robust enough to perform in extremely harsh conditions and could fulfil a range of functions. Then sales and profits started to deteriorate. The firm tried everything it could: new management, changes in pricing, updated specifications, advertising campaigns and so on. To no avail.*

It was only when they stepped back from the numbers and took a fundamental look at the business that the true picture emerged. A separate onshore market for testing equipment had emerged, with a need for simpler and less expensive machines. A competitor had spotted this emerging customer need and had innovated by developing a product specially for this growing segment. It was produced to a simpler specification and lower quality than the existing product. The market leader was stuck in the by now declining offshore sector, while the innovator had established a strong lead in the growing onshore market.

This and countless other examples illustrate the need to look at the market with open, unblinkered eyes. Experience and data are absolutely vital to the efficient running of any mature business. Once in a while, however, the firm has to cast aside its experience and all the lessons it has learned in the past. It has to leave the market research on the shelf and ask some pretty fundamental questions. Who are our customers? Why do they buy? What do they buy? What would they really like to buy? What are we really selling? Why? How does it differ from our competitors? And so on. To be at all worthwhile, the process has to be exhaustive – and exhausting. Nothing must be accepted at face value. Every single assumption must be checked and rechecked. Internal inconsistencies in the logic must be resolved. These inconsistencies are clues, valuable pointers: they show that something is amiss. They must be resolved. Challenge the map.

- **Maintaining the focus:** market knowledge and experience are great assets. They are, however, only of value in markets about which you know something. Far too many mature firms attempt to innovate outside the familiar territory of their core business. It is only too easy to assume that concepts which work in one market will be relevant in another one. Often the superficial similarities which exist can disguise deeper and more fundamental differences. Sometimes it works. Often, however, it does not. Probably the most common situation of all is to try to innovate in some market which has some vague and tenuous link with the core business. 'Synergy' is usually wheeled in to provide the strategic logic for the move. A long list is drawn up of all the potential benefits which will flow to the base business from the new venture and vice versa.

A word of warning: synergy is a much overplayed concept. It

frequently does not deliver any of the supposed benefits and, when it does, they can often be far smaller than originally imagined. There are strong analogies here with the success or otherwise of acquisitions. Synergy is often the route by which acquirers expect value to be created within the combined entity. The track record on mergers and takeovers is well documented: very few of them create any value for the acquirer's shareholders. Most of the supposed value from synergy fails to materialize. In some cases even the opposite can be true: value can be destroyed by the combination.

It is very tempting for the mature firm to believe that its knowledge and experience will have great value in a wide range of areas. This is seldom true. Mature firms which innovate successfully tend to do so in the areas they know best – Sony in consumer electronics, British Steel in speciality steels, Citibank in financial services. Stick to the core.

All of this is not to say that innovation in new business areas is impossible or even inadvisable for mature firms. There are isolated examples of spectacular success from adopting such an approach. What it does suggest however, is that the chances of success are far greater in familiar territory. The main thrust for a company's innovative efforts should always be in the businesses and markets which it knows best. By all means have some more speculative ventures in other attractive but less familiar areas – but accept them for precisely what they are: speculative ventures. Do not attempt to make them the main thrust of the company's innovation programme.

Contacts and credibility

These can provide an extremely powerful advantage in testing and introducing new concepts. Just as in the case of market knowledge, however, this is only truly relevant in the firm's core areas of strength. It is a very appealing and seductive argument for the mature firm to believe that its size or reputation will be of importance to potential customers across a wide spectrum. Generally, they will not. What really matter are relationships between individuals and customers' experience of the firm's competence as a supplier or business partner. These considerations immediately focus attention back onto the company's core businesses and strong customer relationships – and away from more speculative and marginal areas.

There are, of course, conflicts here. Attempting to innovate within one's core business maximizes the likelihood of cannibalizing existing sales, and can also introduce the risk of damaging established and valuable relationships. These are legitimate concerns, but can easily be overplayed:

- **Confront the dilemma:** if innovative opportunities exist within the business then, sooner or later, someone will grasp and develop them. There are really very few businesses where an established competitor can hold back innovations for long. To attempt to do so is a double folly. Firstly, if the firm does not innovate, then someone else will. Secondly, there are extremely few firms which cannot gain far more than they could ever lose through innovating: increased market share, improved margins, a more secure competitive position for the long term, etc.

- **Reinforcing the core:** innovation within the firm's core business need not necessarily cannibalize existing sales. Sometimes it will. Sometimes it won't. Innovation is all about creating new customer value. It is about understanding what customers want and need, and how they wish to buy it. Customers typically have a wide range of needs within one area. There may be innovative opportunities to deliver a broader competence to those customers. Which products or services can be added to the current offering, and delivered through similar channels? How can the current offering be adapted and packaged in different ways? Many consistent innovators adopt this approach:

  - *Tyre and exhaust retailer Kwik-Fit has expanded beyond its original areas of operation into menu-based servicing as well as steering and brake repairs. Each new service has been launched through a separate distinct retail chain after extensive testing in a small number of the original outlets. It is continually considering additional services to add to the range. At the same time as broadening the firm's total offering to customers, however, it has maintained tight focus in each of its individual operations.*

  - *Advertising agencies are evolving worldwide into broadly based business services groups, encompassing many aspects of their clients' communications and marketing needs. They are doing this both by acquisition and by setting up new ventures. In part this is a response to some fundamental shifts in their customers' needs. Advertising per se is losing its primacy as other areas of the marketing budget – PR, promotions, direct marketing, design and sponsored programming – grow in importance. Added to this, the growing complexity of the communications and marketing task are increasing the importance of careful coordination. The agencies are delivering new value to their clients by offering the more comprehensive and integrated competence which is now needed.*

■ *Federal Express's innovative approach to small parcel distribution revolutionized the industry, first in the US and now worldwide. It has continued to innovate as it has grown larger. All its major new ventures build upon its core strengths by serving overlapping but distinct market segments.*

★ *Its overnight letter delivery service provides an extremely competitive service for high priority letters. No competitor has the required scale or infrastructure to compete effectively with them in this new service. Some letters which might previously have been carried as (more expensive) packages will now generate rather less revenue as letters. The expansion of the market will compensate for these losses many times over, however. The system-wide benefit to Federal Express will be huge: the new service generates far higher revenues per pound weight carried.*

★ *It provides an express distribution service for spare parts that is tailored to the needs of such companies as Burroughs in computers. A parts warehouse is located next to Federal's hub in Memphis. From there high priority spare parts can be flown out overnight to be delivered anywhere in the US the next morning. Federal has done more than just provide a new service. It has integrated its value chain with that of its major customers, creating a major source of operating economies and added value.*

● **Positioning and involvement:** new concepts can fail and, by so doing, disappoint customers. The risks which this entails for the overall relationship are inseparably linked to *how* the new idea is introduced. In their desire to maintain confidentiality and avoid giving any potentially valuable information to competitors, many firms become obsessively secretive about their new ventures. This means that when the new idea is introduced it is positioned as a *fait accompli*, the finished (and perfect) article. Rather than being asked to try the product or service out and pass judgement on it, customers are presented with it as the answer to their needs. The firm's reputation is riding on it. Any disappointment is transferred immediately from the new product to the company. Any failing in the product is perceived to be a failing in the company.

How much more productive – and less risky – to involve important and established customers from an early stage in the process. They are then far less likely to be disappointed in the event of failure, and have an interest in contributing to the venture's success (see Chapter 6, Involving the Customer).

Testing the water

Mature companies can often test new concepts at lower cost than the start-up firm. Their existing operations can provide the basic infrastructure upon which to try out the new idea on a marginal basis. Most mature firms recognize these opportunities, but few appreciate their potential extent, or exploit them to the full.

Most innovations rest upon two or three basic hypotheses about what customers value and how they behave. While the ultimate test of the innovation is clearly to launch the new concept fully, it is frequently possible to test the hypotheses in a preliminary way without going to this extent. By so doing, the risks involved in the full launch can be reduced. All innovators make mistakes. They fall into two varieties – cheap ones and expensive ones. Testing innovative hypotheses on a marginal basis gives mature firms a major advantage: the ability to make sure that more of their mistakes are cheap ones.

A testing process like this works most readily in multi-location businesses, where each branch has reasonably uniform operations and lay-out: retail, consumer finance, distribution, etc. In these businesses several new ideas can be tested simultaneously across a number of outlets. Not only does it enable the innovation to be evaluated quickly and at low cost (often with only limited adverse impact on the existing business) but the idea can be rapidly rolled out to other outlets if it proves successful.

■ *One retail group has over three hundred high street outlets. At any one time they are typically testing up to three new concepts in each of five to ten outlets. In some cases this can be done alongside the existing business, while in others it requires dedicating an outlet to the new concept for a period. Thus the firm has a continuous process of experimenting with innovative new ideas, but interferes with the running of only five per cent of its outlets at any one time.*

Mature firms have several inherent advantages in the search for innovation. Exploiting these advantages is the critical first step in improving their chances of success. It has implications for both how they should look for innovation, and in what areas.

REMOVING THE BARRIERS

Perceiving the need for innovation

The first disadvantage which mature firms often face – perceiving the need for innovation – is in some senses the most basic and deeply seated. It relates to the conceptual map with which the firm operates: how does it see its environment and its own role within it? It is a fundamental question of corporate culture and, as such, can be difficult to change. The more successful the company, the stronger the culture tends to be. Culture can seldom be managed or changed directly: it is a derivative of several other aspects of the firm. It is upon those other aspects that management can take action.

The first important task is to raise the profile of innovation within the organization at large. This can be done through a range of communication and motivation actions:

- **Focus on change:** very few markets are mature for long periods. Sooner or later change is needed in the way in which customers receive the value they need. Moreover, there are normally pockets of unsatisfied customer demand scattered around the market: these are potential innovation points. The managers running the business should be encouraged to identify the areas of unsatisfied needs and the potential for creating improved customer value. This should be done in an absolute sense – even if there is no immediate prospect of the firm (or its competitors) being able to deliver that value. At the very least, this should force managers to understand fully their customers' motivations and real needs. They should be encouraged to document the initiatives which competitors are taking. Ideally, this should include an examination of what is going on in foreign markets, if this is possible. Particular emphasis should be placed on those approaches which are targeted on specific segments. They may appear insignificant at the moment, but many innovations start in one segment before migrating to others over time. More generally, an emerging pattern in innovations is that they target customer needs in an ever more segmented and focused manner. In industries from steel to computer systems, niche operators are of increasing importance, and are gaining share from more broadly based competitors.

It is easy to ignore foreign markets as a source of ideas. They can, however, be a double source of opportunity: introducing new approaches into one's own market, or taking proven domestic ideas international. There are opportunities in most industries:

■ *British hotel chains have historically been focused on the middle and upper price segments. In mainland Europe and the US, by contrast, there is a wide range of lodging concepts to suit all kinds of budget. It is only recently that hoteliers (most notably Novotel with its Formula 1 chain) have introduced reasonable quality budget hotels to the UK. Beyond this price-based segmentation, European hoteliers have yet to offer any of the all-suite hotel concepts which have become so popular in the US.*

■ *Fast-track building techniques have been used in the US for many years. In this approach, construction starts on the foundations and lower floors of a multi-storey building before the design details of the upper floors have been finalized (the logic being that one doesn't really need to know what window frames will be used on the twenty-sixth floor in order to put the piling in). It can cut down construction time significantly and, with it, costs. The technique has only recently been introduced to Europe.*

Examining foreign markets and competitors' actions at home and abroad does more, however, than simply provide managers with a source of innovative ideas. It can, at a much more fundamental level, destroy the myth of the mature market with no scope or need for innovation. It can change the way in which managers see their own markets. It should ideally be done as part of the company's regular planning cycle.

● **Measuring innovation:** short-term operating improvements are vital to any business. Focusing on them only becomes dangerous when it is done to the exclusion of exploring new ways of doing business. Short-term performance will always have a major advantage in the competition for management attention: it is constantly measured and reported on. How many companies explicitly measure their innovative performance? Very few. The simple action of actually monitoring attempts at innovation – not only those ideas which are pursued but also those which are proposed but rejected – has a significant effect.

Innovation is brought into the regular reporting cycle. As soon as managers have to report on something – even without being overtly rewarded for their performance – it assumes a greater importance in their thinking. Fundamentally, most people like to perform well. If their individual and collective performance in innovation is measured, this fact alone will signal its importance to the organization. They will start to think more carefully about new ways of delivering customer value. Bringing innovation into the regular reporting cycle is a vital step in raising it in managers' consciousness. Nothing complicated is required, simply a statement to answer these questions:

- How does the firm currently deliver the value that its customers need?

- What are the strengths and weaknesses inherent in this system? What basic customer needs are not addressed?

- What approaches are being considered and tested to deliver value in new ways?

- **Cannibalization:** the perceived risk of cannibalizing existing business with innovations can be an insidious danger to companies' performance. It has led many market leaders to attempt to protect doomed technologies against new and superior solutions. The result is always the same. The tide may be stemmed for a while, but eventually the company loses out to the new initiative:

  - *Du Pont was once the clear leader in the US tyre cord industry with nylon products. As nylon grew to become a major business for the company, it was established as a separate profit centre. Its goal was to maximize Du Pont's returns from its investment in the nylon business. As part of this strategy the Nylon Department established a tyre cord development centre to strengthen this part of the business further.*

    Elsewhere within the corporation polyester fibres were being developed. Their potential in tyres was correctly identified, but – and this was the critical error – was pursued through the Nylon Department's tyre development centre. With their massive investment in nylon research and production capacity, they held back from pushing and exploiting polyester fully. Progress was slow.

    Celanese, meanwhile, had no nylon business to protect. It too recognized polyester's potential and pursued the opportunity vigorously. Although the overall market for tyre cords was static, Celanese's polyester product almost entirely substituted Du Pont's nylon within a five-year period. By the late 1960s Du Pont had lost its dominant position: Celanese had captured 75 per cent of the market.

An isolated tale? Unfortunately not. Companies time and again believe that their currently strong market position can protect them from new and innovative approaches. It seldom does for long. The remedy is to attack the problem at two levels:

■ At the most fundamental level, the inevitability of change and the futility of trying to suppress it must be recognized and communicated. This is bound to be a slow process, and even a painful one. It requires humility and openness. The more successful the firm the more difficult this will be. (Goethe was right to say 'Security is mortal's chiefest enemy.') The challenge is to think like a small firm. Be a challenger, even when you are the leader.

■ At a more practical level, changes to the organization structure may be needed. Vested interests lie at the root of the problem. If Du Pont's tyre cord business had been run as a separate SBU, rather than as part of its nylon business, then its reaction to the polyester opportunity would probably have been different. Wherever possible companies should organize themselves along customer rather than internal (e.g. functional or technological) definitions. By so doing, the firm can ensure that management's attentions are focused on customers' needs. The risks of becoming locked into one particular approach or technology are thereby minimized. (The words 'wherever possible' are important, however. Sometimes, a particular technology or functional specialization may be critical to the firm's competitive advantage. In such cases it may be dangerous to move to a different structure. Careful tradeoffs are needed, depending upon the dynamics of each individual situation.)

● **Broaden the perspective:** firms define their own roles in the market – their mission statement, if you like. The strategic definition chosen for the business may be an abstract concept. It is, however, one with profound implications. It determines every action that the company takes. As markets mature, it is natural to adopt a narrow definition of the business: desire for greater efficiency encourages this view. Such narrowness is limiting however. It disguises the need or scope for innovation: most significant innovations break across existing definitions, rather than optimize within established structures. It is only by adopting a broad and customer-led perspective that firms can unlock a broad recognition of the need for innovation.

Generating the ideas

Once the firm has started to take on board the great opportunities which exist in any business to create new customer value, the innovation process can begin in earnest. It must generate innovative ideas. Here again mature firms face certain disadvantages. Some of these have been discussed already in the previous section: a narrow business definition and a functionally driven organization are common impediments within mature firms. The steps prescribed above will tend to increase the flow of ideas in addition to raising the profile of innovation on a more general level. There are, of course, additional factors which tend to limit the flow of new ideas in many companies:

- **Culture:** the mature firm's corporate culture normally incorporates a strong fear of failure. In a stable and predictable environment, this can be healthy. It provides coherence and direction. In a rapidly evolving environment, however, it is disastrous. A high proportion of all innovations will probably fail. Avoiding failure necessarily excludes innovation.

  This phenomenon is well-known, but the cure is far from obvious. One reaction is to simply adopt a 'macho' approach: to accept the risk of failure without changing any other aspects of the way in which the firm approaches new ventures. The result of this is entirely predictable: a headlong dash into a wide range of often ill-conceived new businesses. Normal caution and management controls are discarded in the name of commitment to risk. When things start to go badly wrong the same commitment can discourage top management from taking effective remedial or damage-limiting action. The result: spectacular and expensive failure. Clearly, something better is required. Innovations can fail for one or more of three reasons:

  - an ill-conceived, poorly thought out concept and business plan,

  - poor execution of that business plan, or

  - the simple fact that the key hypotheses and assumptions which underlie the concept are not borne out in practice.

The third factor is one of the inescapable risks associated with innovation: there will always be uncertainties involved in pursuing a new concept. The first two are not. They are a result of lax management and, as such, should not be tolerated. Careful planning and evaluation of the concept prior to proceeding with it can minimize the risks here. The responsibilities rest within different levels in the organization:

- It is top management which must accept and approve the proposal. Theirs is the responsibility to question and probe the strategic logic underlying the concept and the soundness of the plan. It is their job to identify the critical uncertainties and hypotheses upon which it rests. They will of course rely upon line management to provide the analysis and detail which is required to do so. The ultimate responsibility, however, is theirs and theirs alone. By approving and supporting a new venture they signal their acceptance of the concept and the business plan.

- The line managers running the new venture must develop and then accept the business plan and operate within its confines. They have to deliver. They should not accept responsibility for anything which they do not feel comfortable with. The plan should be precise: it must spell out what resources are available and what is expected of the line managers. It must have clear benchmarks and targets against which their performance can be measured.

There is tremendous value to making the risks involved explicit. Too often companies engage in innovative ventures without a clear understanding of where the key risks and uncertainties lie. It is this lack of clarity and knowledge which make innovation appear to be even more risky than it need be. They increase the fear of failure. Explicitly identifying and measuring the risks makes them more manageable, and therefore acceptable. It reduces one of the barriers to innovation.

Once this has been done, the venture may still fail. If it does, the reasons for that failure must be analysed – honestly and rigorously. This is not a witch-hunt, however. It is part of the normal system of management control which should exist within all organizations, innovative or otherwise. If the reasons really are part of the inherent risk of innovating, then that must be clearly and unambiguously stated and communicated within the organization. Nobody is to blame. If, however, the failure is due either to the acceptance of an unsound plan, or to the poor execution of that plan, then the business failure is also a management failure. Appropriate action should be taken. It is only by doing this that performance the next time can be improved.

- **People:** the people who join and progress with mature companies are unlikely to be entrepreneurs at heart. That much is inescapable. In every large organization, however, there are always some managers who have many of the requisite talents. They are waiting for an opportunity to use them. The trick is how to spot and encourage them. Standard career paths within mature companies seldom help: the surest way to ensure promotion is to turn in a steady performance in a well-defined role. There is often little to be gained and potentially much to lose from being involved in risky new ventures.

  The remedy is to bring innovation into the standard career path. Starting and running new ventures must become a viable alternative to the more typical options available. Specifically, the ideal system should:

  - reward (monetarily or otherwise) successful innovators;

  - accept failure, where this is due to the inherent risks of innovating (but not otherwise);

  - have the flexibility to allow managers to return to a role within the existing organization after a period of running a new venture. (They will probably be better managers anyway for having had this experience.)

Introducing these changes will not transform the mature firm overnight, and relatively few of its managers will ever become really skilled entrepreneurs. What they can do, however, is to remove some of the inbuilt barriers and biases which prevent mature firms from maximizing their potential. They can form a major strand in the firm's innovation strategy:

- *3M provides an excellent example of how new ventures can be incorporated within standard career structures. The firm is continuously innovative, forever introducing and testing new concepts. It has clearly stated goals for what proportion of sales revenue should come from products launched within the previous five years. Running a new venture is fully accepted as part of the normal career structure for rising managers. Individuals are able to spend a proportion of their time pursuing their own pet projects, provided their main responsibilities are under control. The firm has a deep understanding of the risks involved in innovating: failure of a new venture need not unreasonably damage a manager's career.*

- **Integration:** successful innovation requires adopting an integrated view of customers' needs, and how value can be delivered to them. Tight functional responsibilities – while often necessary to ensure maximum efficiency – hamper managers from adopting such an integrated view. There is clearly a natural tension here between the two conflicting desires of integrating and dividing responsibilities. In many cases it will be unrealistic to attempt to achieve full integration across all relevant functions on a continuous day-to-day basis. The penalties in terms of increased complexity and lost efficiency may be too great. In these circumstances it may be most appropriate to convene cross-functional teams of managers to develop innovative approaches to the business. This should be done in parallel with their regular line responsibilities. Who should be involved? How many managers should be in the team? Commonsense dictates that a few simple rules should be adhered to:

  ▪ The team should be composed primarily of line managers, retaining their everyday responsibilities. This is needed to retain a practical perspective.

  ▪ It must contain managers representing each of the functions which are most critical to the success of the business, in addition to a general manager.

  ▪ The team should be small enough to enable creative team dynamics to work effectively. As a general rule, five or six people should be the maximum.

  ▪ Its members should be drawn from the organization's current and likely future leaders. It must retain a commitment to excellence.

  ▪ Finally, there can be more than one team, if management resources permit this. Different teams can either focus on distinct areas, or they can proceed in competition with each other: both approaches can yield excellent results.

Evaluating the opportunity

Once the firm is starting to generate innovative ideas, they will have to be evaluated and subsequently approved or rejected. Many mature firms employ evaluation methods which are not only poor at choosing between proposals, but also tend to push the overall innovation effort in one particular direction: towards low-risk and only marginally innovative ventures. The remedy is to ensure that the evaluation is being done in a fundamentally strategic manner, explicitly isolating the new value which is being created, rather than focusing primarily on financial projections (see Chapter 5, Evaluating the Opportunity).

Implementing innovation

Mature firms have historically tended to also have problems in the implementation phase of their innovations. The major reasons were identified earlier. Individually they act as important barriers. Together they form a vicious circle, seriously impairing the firm's innovative performance. The circle has to be broken. Not all these factors apply to every mature firm, of course, but in most cases at least two or three will. Direct action can be taken to minimize or remove each one as a negative factor:

- **The light hand:** the new venture should not be over-resourced, nor should it have to operate within the constraints of the parent organization. Both of these pitfalls are a manifestation of the same underlying tendency: to run the new venture like a mature business. It is not. New ventures are fundamentally different and should be treated as such. To draw them too closely to the structure, culture and systems of the parent organization is dangerous in the extreme. It encourages behaviour traits which are counter-productive to the new venture's success. It also introduces added constraints and gives vested interests the opportunity to make their influence felt. New ventures will always cause conflicts to one degree or another. That is inevitable. These conflicts must not be allowed to hamper its progress. If necessary, the new business should be set up as an independent entity. Sometimes it may even be in competition with the parent company.

    Too many firms believe that they can avoid these conflicts by making tradeoffs and compromises at a high level. They cannot. All this will do is to hamper severely the new venture's prospects and –

equally significant – inhibit the parent company's response to the innovation. Instead of taking positive action to address the real strategic issues head-on, the organization incorrectly assumes that the negotiated compromise has resolved the issue:

- *Du Pont assumed that it could hold back polyester's development as a tyre cord material until its nylon production capacity was fully utilized. Celanese proved them wrong. It cost Du Pont its leadership of the tyre cord market.*

- *A leading financial services company had experimented with direct distribution of its products. By doing so it could cut out the need for intermediaries and, with them, its expensive branch network. The cost savings were major. The tests went well – customers liked the simplicity and improved quality of service which dealing directly could offer.*

  Only one problem. The branch managers were a powerful body in the organization, and blocked the new move. A compromise was reached. The product could be advertised centrally but the enquiries generated would be sent to the branches for follow-up, and then returned to the centre for further administration and documentation. The results were entirely predictable: higher costs and slower service.

  After some years of operating this way the company finally took the plunge and went to a central, fully automated system. In the meantime, however, the lead had passed to a competitor, who now has a dominant position in this emerging sector of the business. (Incidentally, there is an interesting twist to the tale: the new competitor is from outside the industry. He had no entrenched position to protect, and went straight to a centralized solution.)

There really is little alternative: to succeed, the managers running the new venture must be given complete freedom to pursue the opportunity in whatever way they choose. Anything less constitutes an unacceptable millstone.

- **The role of top management:** once the firm has embarked on a new venture the role of the parent company should be that of coach, not policeman. Decision-making must be as rapid as possible. Day-to-day decisions should be the clear responsibility of the managers of the new venture itself. Top management in the parent company should only be involved in major strategic questions, in particular those involving additional finance or resources.

  Possibly even more critical than the speed with which decisions are taken is the nature of those decisions. Parent company management all too often see their role as that of controlling the new venture (as in the financial services example above). It should not be. The real value which top management can add is in supporting the new venture – with strategic guidance as well as finance. In a sense their ideal role can be compared to that of a venture capitalist, but one who can add value in a much wider range of areas than is normal:

- a deep understanding of the market

- the ability to assist the new venture by virtue of its contacts and reputation

- a facility to try out new ideas on a marginal cost basis

- a longer-term perspective on the investment and the time during which a return must be earned.

By adopting this position the parent company can give its new ventures a competitive edge which few, if any, independent start-ups enjoy. Its role should be that of coach, not policeman.

- **Accepting defeat:** one of the most underplayed yet vital aspects of innovation is knowing when to accept defeat and abandon the project. Few companies do this soon enough. The real challenge is to do this effectively – yet without interfering with the day-to-day decision making of the new venture. A delicate touch is needed.

  The evaluation method used can play a major role here. It should concentrate on the strategic factors behind the innovation. Exactly what is the new value that is being created for customers? What are the uncertainties involved? A clear and unambiguous statement of this is invaluable. Producing one should be an integral part of the evaluation process. It provides management with an acid test of the project's viability as and when problems arise. Do the key foundations of the innovation still hold? If so, there is probably a way around the problems. If not, there probably is not. Then is the time to withdraw, not when the red ink has grown to completely unacceptable levels.

Changing the culture

The principal barrier faced by mature firms is a cultural one. It is difficult to change this directly. Conversely, superficial changes to the culture without improvements in all the detailed aspects of how

Figure 23: Innovating in mature firms: building on strength and minimizing weaknesses

Building on strength	Minimizing weaknesses

Knowledge of the market
• Stick to markets you know
• Avoid myopia
  ▪ periodic fundamental review of conceptual maps
Contacts and credibility
• Involve the customer
Testing new concepts
• Exploit opportunities for testing key hypotheses on a marginal basis
	Perceiving the need for innovation
	• Destroy the myth of the 'mature market'
	• Monitor innovation efforts
	• Adopt broad definition of firm's role
	  ▪ customer focus
	Generating innovative ideas
	• Culture: acceptance of failure
	  ▪ segregate risks
	• Bring innovation into the standard career path
	• Integrate inputs from all key functions
	  ▪ teamwork (small teams)
	Evaluating innovative ideas
	• Strategic focus
	Implementing innovative ideas
	• Organize to limit the influence of vested interests
	  ▪ independence
	• Avoid over-resourcing
	• Minimize restraints
	• Rapid decision-making
	• The corporation as venture capitalist and coach
	• Prepared to abandon if appropriate

managers look for, evaluate and implement innovative ideas are worth little. Culture in the true sense is the integration of all the detailed actions which managers take, how the organization thinks and functions. It is these which are amenable to change. It is these which can be managed directly. Figure 23 summarizes the actions which management can take to minimize the firm's inherent weaknesses, and build upon its strengths. Each one is important in itself. Each one can have a significant payoff for the firm. Together, however, they are even more important. Making the detailed changes soon flows through to change the culture itself. Managed correctly, they become the catalyst to change the firm's innovative style, strategy and performance.

Mature firms are rarely as innovative as they should be. They operate under certain inherent disadvantages. But they have strengths too. They can transform their performance by building on those strengths and minimizing the weaknesses. By doing so, they can start to build a more innovative culture. The debate as to whether mature firms will ever be as innovative as young ones is as intractable as it is academic. The incontrovertible fact remains: they have to improve their performance. It can be done.

SUMMARY

Innovation is the key challenge facing mature firms today.

Mature firms have inherent strengths and weaknesses in the quest for innovation.

Building on those strengths and minimizing weaknesses has major positive effects:

- Directly: improves the quality of specific decisions and actions
- Indirectly: cumulative effect on the firm's culture.

11 INNOVATION AND THE YOUNG FIRM

Young firms have historically been the most successful innovators. Many of them become victims of their own success, however.

The most vital – and difficult – quality to maintain is focus. It is only by focusing resolutely on its strategic core that the innovative young firm can realize its potential. Pursuing too many opportunities guarantees failure.

11 INNOVATION AND THE YOUNG FIRM

- The track record

- Choosing the core

- The high margin, high overhead trap

- Planning for setbacks

- Setting the pace

- Finding the finance

- The international options

THE TRACK RECORD

The archetypal innovative firm is the new start-up, setting out to develop some brilliant new concept. Ask most people to describe the ideal innovative environment and they will talk of small teams, entrepreneurs, risk-taking, meritocracy and freedom from vested interests and organizational constraints. The evidence supports this popular view:

- Every survey of employment confirms the rapid growth of small firms. The vast majority of new jobs created in the past decade have come from small companies. Large corporations account for a declining proportion of total employment. This is true at the individual company level as well as in the economy in general. US firms which in 1969 had fewer than 20 employees and which still existed in 1976 had an average employment growth of over 26 per cent during the period. The corresponding figure for firms with over 500 employees was a 6 per cent decline. Now, this difference can be explained partly by the growth in service, as opposed to manufacturing industries, but a significant part was due to successful innovation by the smaller companies.

- Most surveys of relative financial performance show that small firms do better than large ones on average. Over a long period, Britain's USM companies have outperformed those on the main exchange. Various stock indices focused on smaller companies have shown excellent growth. (It is interesting to consider this fact alongside the generally higher failure rates among small firms. Given that the *average* performance of small firms is superior, then the performance of those that survive must be better by an even larger margin.)

- A huge number of truly significant innovations have been brought to the market by start-up companies. Many of them have gone on to become leading players in their industry:

  ■ *Apple Computers began in Steven Jobs' garage.*

  ■ *Federal Express was the largest US start-up ever when it was launched in 1971.*

  ■ *People Express started out in 1981 with three used Boeing 737s.*

  ■ *Tie Rack was founded with two shops in 1979 by entrepreneur Roy Bishko.*

  ■ *Sea Containers was a start-up run by three partners when it entered the container leasing business.*

  ■ *Kwik-Fit started with one outlet in 1971.*

CHOOSING THE CORE

Despite all the successes, innovation is still very risky for young firms. A high proportion of all start-ups fail within the first few years. Innovation has to be properly managed to control the risks. Many of the guidelines discussed in the previous chapter are relevant to start-ups. Young firms, however, face particular challenges.

If there is one quality which young innovative companies need more than any other it is focus. They simply have less time and resources to play with than most mature firms. They cannot possibly hope to pursue all the attractive leads and opportunites which arise – for not only would this spread their resources too thinly, it would also require a management so complex that it would swamp the growing firm.

It is in the very nature of most young firms, because of their culture, their people and all the feedback they get from the market, to be highly adaptive rather than to focus on a clear core. Without careful focus the firm can easily find itself chasing far too many opportunities (see Chapter 14, Adaptive and Repetitive Behaviour). The more successful the innovation, the greater the problem. Potential customers from many different areas want to try the product. They all need something slightly different. The growing company obliges. Bit by bit, it loses all the focus which it had. Trying to move in too many directions at once it loses all momentum, all sense of direction. The firm becomes a victim of its own success.

To an extent this trauma is inevitable. The more innovative the firm is, the more difficult it is to get the strategy right: there is an unavoidable degree of risk. What the innovative young firm can do is to minimize that risk by focusing tightly on the true strategic core of the business. Too few do, however. Those which focus carefully increase their chances of success dramatically. Most truly successful innovators have taken some quite straightforward concept and have run very hard with it. Conversely, very few young firms which hedge their bets and follow a wide range of opportunities ever achieve much. They simply create the illusion of frenetic activity, but with limited results. You need a core.

Choosing the core areas upon which to focus is rarely difficult. Every innovation affects different users or customers in a distinct way. Some gain more from it than others. Some are more likely to try a new idea early on than others. At heart, this is a question of strategic segmentation. A great deal has been written on this already. The innovator must identify the relevant core segments within the target market and focus resolutely on them. It is only when he has established a truly viable position within the first target segments that he should consider expanding into others. Too early and the firm loses focus and direction. Too late and one misses opportunites. There are no easy answers. The right strategy depends upon each individual situation. Careful analysis is required. Two thoughts are worth bearing in mind, however:

• Every natural tendency of the young firm is to change and adapt rather than focus. If there is serious doubt as to whether the time has arrived to broaden out or not, then that argues strongly in favour of continued focus.

- All the evidence suggests that competitors are slow to copy innovators. Err on the side of caution: continuing to focus longer than is necessary may defer opportunities, but only rarely loses them permanently. Entering new areas too rapidly destroys many firms.

THE HIGH MARGIN, HIGH OVERHEAD TRAP

One specific way in which firms can lose their strategic focus is widespread enough to warrant special mention; the high margin, high overhead trap. It is seductively easy to fall into, very difficult to get out of. It works like this.

The firm has an innovation which is applicable to a broad range of customers – some large, some small, some requiring standard products, others who need slightly modified ones. It has a given level of resources available for selling, customer engineering, service and administration. It views these as fixed overheads.

The firm receives enquiries for sales, which it pursues. The gross margins are best for smaller customers and for those which need slight modifications. Attracted by the gross margins, the firm tries to win more of this type of order. It succeeds. They gradually constitute a higher proportion of sales. Overhead levels rise as more resources are added to cope with the increasing flow of small and non-standard orders.

Before long the firm finds that its overheads are too high for it to compete at the volume end of the market. It has been relegated to the role of a specialist short run-length supplier.

Now, the point of this example is not that being a specialist short run-length supplier is of necessity a bad strategy. For some firms this would be the best option by far. For others, however, it would be completely wrong. Unfortunately many firms *drift* into this position. By failing to determine their strategy in the market these firms abdicate control. Rather than actively exploiting opportunites in the market, they are passively driven by it. It is depressing how many innovative firms lose control in this way:

■ *A small German engineering manufacturer had developed a radically new design of hydraulic motor. The main subassembly in it – the torque unit – was far simpler and cheaper than any competing product. It had 60 per cent fewer moving parts than comparable existing models.*

Potential customers fell broadly into two camps. First, there were large original equipment manufacturers (OEMs) who bought the torque unit alone for assembly into their product. They required relatively little sales effort or technical service. Second, there were the smaller OEMs and end users, who bought the torque unit already built into a complete motor. They required significant sales effort and technical assistance.

■ *Supplying these two types of customer of course required radically different cost structures (Figure 24). Consider the strategic aspects: the company's fundamental advantage lay in the torque unit. In the other motor components and in the sales/technical service it was at a disadvantage compared with the larger players in the industry. In other words, it had a competitive advantage in serving large OEMs, but was disadvantaged in trying to sell to small OEMs and users.*

Figure 24: The innovator often has a competitive advantage only in certain segments. (Hydraulic motors example)

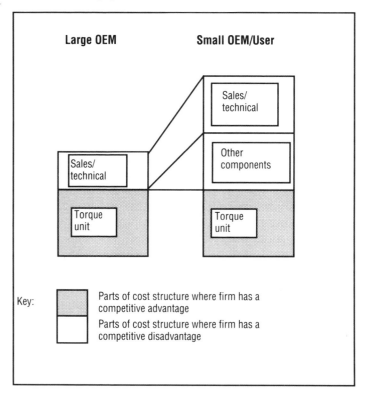

The firm started off with the most appropriate strategy: to focus its efforts on large OEMs. It found that convincing them to use the new motor in large volumes took longer than expected (Chapter 6, Involving the Customer). At the same time, it started getting enquiries from

smaller OEMs and users. These customers were prepared to pay more, but needed more additional service and products. The firm was enticed by the higher prices – after all, it was extremely profitable on a marginal cost basis, wasn't it?

Before long the majority of sales were coming from these customers. The firm added the sales, technical and manufacturing overhead that it needed to serve them. It found that it could no longer compete effectively for the large OEMs' business, where price was a key concern. Unwittingly, it had given away its core strengths and lost its focus. It was trapped. Soon afterwards, the firm folded.

Focus is perhaps the most important attribute for a young innovative firm to achieve. It is certainly the most difficult. There is a continued tension between maintaining focus and responding to customer needs. After all, innovation is all about delivering value to customers. The firm must set its strategy with careful regard to how the customer and the market work – yet it must at all costs avoid reacting to them in a passive way. To do so is to abdicate strategic control. Failure soon follows. Managing tensions is a key attribute for success.

PLANNING FOR SETBACKS

Some of the risks which innovative firms face are avoidable through careful focus. Others are not. It is almost inevitable that the growing firm will make serious mistakes and encounter significant problems along the way. It should plan for these setbacks. At one level this implies nothing more than recognizing that they will happen. It is incredibly easy for management to keep its eye on some far distant goal, and be blind to emerging problems. At another level, it implies keeping something in reserve to tackle the problems, which fall into two varieties: detailed and fundamental ones.

- **Detailed** problems, relating to the day-to-day running of the firm. There is nothing fundamentally wrong with the innovation, but problems have arisen in its implementation. These are often the easiest to detect – firstly, they are visible (customers call to complain, stock piles up in the warehouse etc.) and secondly, most managers, through training and experience, expect to meet such problems in the daily course of events. Such problems are very significant. The number of innovative firms which fail to realize their full potential because obvious problems are not dealt with is depressing. Few have achieved success without passing through some rough patches along the way. (Federal Express went through dire cash flow problems during its first four years, Kwik-Fit's administration system nearly ground to a halt when it grew too fast.) The novelty and high growth rate which typify the start-up firm mean that problems arise quickly. There is often little time to set things back on course once more.

- **Fundamental** problems are often more difficult to detect. They relate to some basic flaw in the concept behind the innovation. They bar it from delivering the customer value which it sets out to do. Sometimes they are insuperable. Often, however, some change to the configuration or delivery of the product or service will save the situation.

The main difficulty lies not so much in resolving the problem as in identifying it in the first place. The stronger and more committed the innovator is to his concept, the more difficult it is to accept that it may need significant revision. In fact, this is the mirror image of the problem which the established competitor often has in recognizing the value of the innovation. The innovator's conceptual map indicates that the business and customer work in a particular way, and that the innovation interacts with them in a specific manner. When things do not work out as planned, the first reaction is to assume the problem is due to conservatism among buyers/poor selling/the need for a bit more development/etc. Anything, in fact, other than a wholesale revision of the basic concept. It is extremely difficult to accept the need for a new conceptual map.

There is a remedy. If the planning and evaluation of the venture have been done properly, then there should be a clear strategic statement of what the innovation is, how it delivers customer value and what critical assumptions underlie it. This should be written down in a concise form. There should be no redundancies or ambiguities in it: if any part of the statement is invalidated, it should raise serious questions about the viability of the whole innovation. Producing such a statement has tremendous value. It forces the strategic thinking onto a new level. Ideas and concepts which can remain hazy in the mind become crystallized when written down. Inconsistencies and vague statements become immediately apparent.

This statement is an extemely valuable management tool when starting a new venture. Its true worth comes in identifying fundamental problems early on. Management should revisit the statement on a regular basis and ask whether recent experience confirms or refutes any part of it. Done conscientiously, this is a powerful control mechanism. It need not take much time – half an hour of careful thought every two months or so is often sufficient. The payoff can be enormous: it helps to separate problems into the detailed and the truly fundamental.

SETTING THE PACE

Allied to the issues of focus and planning for setbacks is the question of the rate of development. Every natural instinct tends to encourage the innovator to grow as rapidly as possible, to go for the jackpot. This is driven partly by a natural desire to grow, and partly by a logical concern to establish a secure position before competitors can react. Against this must be placed the risks of failure incurred by too rapid an expansion programme. There is a natural tension here. Few firms resolve it in the best way.

Figure 25 shows some of the key tasks and risks involved as the young innovative firm develops. For the sake of simplicity the firm's development is divided into three stages: proving the concept, building the system, growing the business. In practice, of course, the three stages overlap to a considerable degree. The table makes the case for a **slow-fast** approach to innovative development for small firms:

- **Proving the concept:** the first critical task which the firm faces is to test and refine the basic concept behind the innovation. To be worthwhile this must be done carefully and thoroughly: time spent here will pay tremendous dividends later. There is no need to rush: if it is a truly innovative concept the competitors are quite likely to ignore or rationalize it away, assuming they notice it in the first place. A slow approach works best: care and patience are needed.
  Far too many innovators ignore or skim over this stage, in their rush to grow. Generally they pay the price later.

- **Building the system:** the second stage is arguably the most difficult to gauge correctly. The young firm must build a team and a business system which will help it to move onto the next phase of rapid growth. Ideally, this should take time. Sometimes the competitors are still unlikely to pick the innovation up at this stage. If that is judged to be the case, the firm should again progress slowly and carefully in building up its base. Sometimes, however, there is a real risk of competitive entry at this point. If that is thought to be the case, then

Figure 25: The challenges which the young firm faces as it develops its innovation

	Key tasks	Risks faced by the firm		Appropriate rate of development
		Internal	Competitive	
I Proving the concept	Ensuring that the concept and hypotheses underlying the innovation are valid	High • Failure adequately to test and refine the concept can undermine the venture	Low • Good chance that competitors will be unaware of the innovation, or will ignore it	Slow • Worth taking time to get it right
II Building the system	Building a team and a business system to enable the firm to operate effectively and to grow	High • Failure to build a sound base will cause severe problems later on	Low-High • Sometimes competitors will ignore the innovation. Sometimes competitors will start to respond by this stage	Difficult choice • depends on individual situation
III Growing the business	Growing. Establishing a strong position ahead of competitors	Low • If I and II have been done properly growth should entail only limited risks	High • Competitors will increasingly realize the value of innovation and are likely to respond	Fast • Vital to maintain leadership in the market

the firm must move rapidly ahead. It simply has to manage and survive the tensions which this will cause.

Again, few firms get the balance just right. Determining the rate of development calls for careful tradeoffs: they are seldom easy to make.

• **Growing the business:** this stage should generally be pursued rapidly. The firm has by now developed a sound base, and increased competitive pressures are likely to call for rapid development. The more carefully the previous two stages have been completed, the stronger the firm's position to grow rapidly at this stage.

Of course, the terms 'fast' and 'slow' are relative. In a young firm everything happens quickly. If it does not, something is seriously wrong. There is a positive value to always stretching oneself and the firm – staying at the cutting edge. It keeps the excitement up and the ideas flowing. It keeps the firm vital. It is in this context that one should deliberately take enough time, but keep things moving.

FINDING THE FINANCE

Finance is usually high on the list of concerns for young firms. It is, however, less of an issue today than it once was. There is generally more money available than there are good original business ideas. A viable new concept can usually find the backing it needs. The concern which innovators should have is not so much how to raise finance, but how to raise it on the best possible terms.

Many of them ignore what can potentially be the most attractive sources of finance. They approach all the obvious sources – banks, venture capitalists and other investors. These sources have a purely financial interest – they put money in, and expect to get money out. They have no broader interest or involvement in the new venture. All innovations affect a number of players, however, principally suppliers and customers. They often have a strong business interest in supporting the new venture, since it benefits them directly. They may be prepared to invest. Because of their interest, they usually have less onerous expectations than other types of investor in terms of the straight financial return required. This can result in a better deal for the innovator. The message is clear: actively seek out investors with strong business reasons for helping to finance the new venture. Several successful innovators have followed this route:

- *Sea Containers started out with relatively little capital – certainly less than it needed to start building up a fleet of containers for leasing out. The firm found an established steel fabricator in Germany which was keen to diversify into what it saw as a growth area. Sea Containers was able to negotiate unusually favourable payment terms on the containers it purchased, thus reducing its needs for working capital.*

- *Kwik-Fit's expansion was helped by the tyre and exhaust manufacturers. They recognized the potential value to them of this new distribution channel. Their confidence in Tom Farmer and the firm's future led them to finance the required stock by extending good credit terms.*

- *Many large communications, marketing services and financial groups wish to expand their activities into the growing consulting market. Several start-up firms have received financial backing from these groups.*

THE INTERNATIONAL OPTIONS

Finally, internationalization should be a high priority for many young innovative firms, even at an early stage. Improvements in communications and the media are making markets worldwide converge ever more. Global competition and marketing are gathering pace. In many instances – although by no means all – new concepts which succeed in one market are likely to do well in another. The true payoff to an innovation can come from exploiting it internationally, not just in one market.

Historically, many innovations have in fact been quite slow to migrate from one market to another (Chapter 4, Looking for Innovation). This has often given their developers ample opportunity to establish the business soundly in one market before taking the idea international. As a result, several major innovations have been rolled out gradually on a worldwide basis by the original company.

This will doubtless remain the case in several areas. Directionally, however, things are changing: businessmen are increasingly aware of the opportunities to take ideas from one market and exploit them elsewhere. Innovators are likely to have an increasingly small window of opportunity in which to exploit their own ideas internationally before a competitor does. Mature companies may have the depth of management and financial resources to do this successfully. For young firms, however, rapid international expansion can cause terrific strain. It has been the downfall of many a firm in the past, and will continue to claim victims. Firms need a way to resolve the tensions which arise in choosing between the risks of over-rapid international expansion on the one hand and losing international opportunities on the other hand. At heart this is another aspect of the conflicts which young firms face in maintaining focus as they expand. In resolving it they should explore all possibilities for capitalizing on their strength (the idea itself, and their intimate understanding of it) while minimizing their relative weaknesses:

- Joint ventures are notoriously difficult to manage but can be of great value if done correctly. Careful use of joint venture arrangements has enabled several firms to expand internationally with success. Licensing is a variation on the same theme.

- In some situations acquisition by a larger group may be the best route from a business development perspective and for the firm's owners and executives.

Young firms have historically been the most successful innovators. Their energy and drive is the greatest asset – and their Achilles heel. Too many promising firms become victims of their own success. Avoiding this requires vigilance and, above all, consciously focusing on the firm's core and taking the time to get the critical aspects of the firm's operations right. This creates tension: every instinct is to rush ahead and try out more new ideas. Successfully managing those tensions is the real key success factor for innovative young firms.

SUMMARY

All firms face the same basic challenges in innovating successfully, but some are particularly important for young firms:

- Focus on the **strategic core** of the business
- Only expand when the core is truly secure
- Avoid **high margin, high overhead traps**
- **Plan for setbacks**
  - **detailed** problems
  - **fundamental** problems
- Adopt a **slow-fast** approach to development
- Exploit **sources of finance** with **strong business reasons for investing**
- **Internationalize** as soon as possible at acceptable risk.

IV INNOVATION IN CONTEXT

12 INNOVATIONS AND INNOVATIVENESS

Individual innovations are important. Alone, however, they are not enough. Companies must become innovative in all that they do – to build innovativeness into all aspects of their operations.

Few companies have a detailed picture of how much they are investing in innovation, in which areas and with what success. Without this information it is impossible to take corrective action. An innovativeness audit is required.

12 INNOVATIONS AND INNOVATIVENESS

- Innovativeness: the management challenge

- Innovative myopia

- Innovativeness: part of the cost of being in business

- Measuring the process: the innovativeness audit

INNOVATIVENESS: THE MANAGEMENT CHALLENGE

Thus far, most of this book has focused on innovations – i.e. the new ideas themselves which can be translated into new business ventures or improved ways of performing in existing ones. Each innovation is considered as a discrete entity. So it is with most companies: the natural focus is on individual concrete opportunities, rather than on the more abstract concept of innovativeness. In most situations this is entirely understandable and indeed desirable. Business, after all, is about identifying and fulfilling real customer needs and not about developing theoretical constructs.

Sometimes, however, it is appropriate for even the most hard-nosed of managements in the most cut-throat of industries to take one step back and consider their company's innovativeness in isolation from any individual innovations. This is exactly analogous to considering the firm's organization structure in isolation from individual managers, or its strategic direction in isolation from individual operating decisions. It is a question of raising the level of debate. The reasons for doing so are compelling. The business environment is evolving more rapidly than ever before. Increased competitive pressures and improved communications are shortening product (and company) life cycles. Deregulation is changing the rules of competition in industries worldwide. Higher standards of corporate information and the City's willingness to back aggressive management are themselves increasing the pressures to perform.

These changes are fundamental. They represent a step-change in the environment within which all firms must compete. All signs are that individual markets, indeed the whole business world, will continue to become more turbulent. This is not a temporary phenomenon. Chaos is here to stay. In this environment, established sources of competitive advantage may no longer continue to guarantee success. The high market share which was so valuable yesterday can easily lose its relevance tomorrow, as markets segment and divide. The low cost position which in the past might have conferred a significant advantage can rapidly evaporate. Large, low cost manufacturing plants can turn into millstones as new technologies or consumer needs emerge. Even success itself can become a straight-jacket, limiting management's ability to embrace new visions. One source of competitive advantage is, however, of increasing importance. It is management itself. Its professionalism, creativity and agility are the most powerful competitive advantages which any firm can have:

- Without them, even what seems to be the most unassailable of positions can rapidly crumble as the fundamentals of the market shift. Industrial archaeology is full of once great companies which failed to adapt.

- With them, even the historically most weak competitor can spot and exploit the opportunities created by shifts in the market.

The premium and rewards to innovative management are steadily increasing. A fundamental goal of managers in all industries should be to make their organizations more innovative in every aspect of their operations. This is a fundamentally different challenge to that of pursuing each innovation per se. Each new idea is a finite entity: it has a beginning, a middle and an end. It can be defined and made real. It can be measured. Innovativeness is different. It is not so much a sequence of innovations as a state of being. It is an integral part of the firm's culture and strategy, part of its very fabric (Figure 26). There is no end point, no finishing post in the race for innovativeness. The best that can be hoped for is a position superior to that of the competition at any point in time: how innovative is the firm compared to its competitors? In most industries even the goal posts are shifting: competitors are recognizing

Figure 26: Innovations can take a company forwards

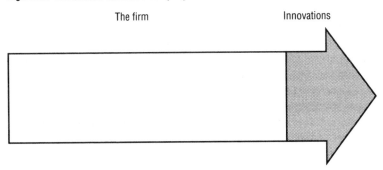

. . . **but innovativeness can take it much further.**

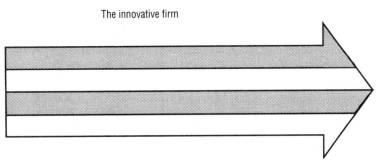

the need to adapt and are themselves becoming more innovative. The firms which win the competitive battle in future will increasingly be those which stay ahead in the race for innovativeness. The real winners will be those who can hone and improve their innovative skills more rapidly than their competitors. Relative performance will be the true determinant of success. Some of the most successful companies distinguish themselves more by their innovativeness than by any innovations per se:

■ *Pepsi and Coca Cola have been locked in combat for decades – the 'Cola Wars'. By and large, Pepsi has been the more innovative company – not just in terms of major new product launches like Diet Pepsi with Nutrasweet or Slice with real fruit juice, but in every aspect of its organization and operations. As a result, Pepsi has inexorably closed the gap with Coca Cola in the US market. Coca Cola behaves like a leader. Pepsi is the challenger.*

■ *The greatest single innovation in the automobile industry since the Second World War – indeed in manufacturing industry as a whole – has been the Toyota Production System. The concept is brilliantly simple: cars can actually be produced efficiently on a production line with small batches and where each part or assembly arrives in the right place at the right time with no need for wasteful inventory. Making the concept a reality took 30 years. 30 years of the whole corporation becoming attuned to the new production system, developing it further as it progressed. 30 years of continuous innovative effort.*

INNOVATIVE MYOPIA

Far too many companies still focus on individual innovations at the expense of a broader innovativeness. This has many unfortunate consequences. By their discrete nature, individual innovations can be considered in isolation from the ongoing management of the business itself. Managers can think of innovations as additions to the firm, rather than as an integral part of it. To the extent that this does happen, it encourages the view that innovation should indeed be separated from the day-to-day running of the business. At its worst, this can lead to innovation being driven out of the mainstream of the organization and into a separate group responsible for 'new ventures'. Occasionally, such an approach might work – such as to develop a specific new product. Normally, however, the results are disastrous:

● The 'new ventures' department becomes isolated from the mainstream of the business. It loses all appreciation of customers' real needs, as well as the problems and opportunities which arise on a day-to-day basis in running the business. These daily events are real 'moments of truth'. They contain the seeds of innovative ideas. Without access to them the flow of new concepts can dry up. At best, the new ventures department's performance is hampered by the organizational and cultural barriers which grow between it and the rest of the company. At worst it becomes completely aloof, isolated and ineffective.

● At the same time, the rest of the organization begins to take its eye off the ball: it abdicates responsibility for innovation to the new ventures group. Instead, it concentrates on the day-to-day efficient running of the business. Without a responsibility for and commitment to innovation, the firm risks becoming blind to the opportunities and new ideas which continually arise during the normal cut and thrust of business. On those few occasions where managers from within the business itself do develop and push new ideas they receive only negative feedback. They risk finding that the new ventures department will either block the idea or attempt to take it over. Not surprisingly, the flow of new ideas dries up:

■ *One engineering firm had a strong corporate R&D centre. Over the years this department had assumed responsibility for all new ventures. Its fundamental outlook remained that of the research department, however. Its key goals seemed to be meticulously proving results and publishing interesting findings. Satisfying customer needs was less important. The firm had made a fundamental mistake in confusing research with innovation.*

Line managers found that their development ideas got tied up in a morass of science and red tape. The flow of new products slowed to a trickle. Once renowned for its excellent products, the firm fell behind its competitors. It failed to introduce new manufacturing methods, so its costs and prices fell out of line with the market. The firm inexorably declined until it was serving only a small segment of the market – those customers who were insensitive to price and performance insensitive customers. It was living off its brand name, slowly liquidating its business.

It eventually rid itself of the R&D centre. Performance did improve. The damage, however, had been done – the firm was a shadow of its former self.

Considering each innovation as a separate, self-contained entity tends to focus attention on the individually great opportunities, the big shots. While these are indeed critically important, they are only the tip of the iceberg. There is usually a myriad of smaller ideas to be tried, and improvements to be made. Taken together they can radically alter the firm and its performance. The only way to ensure that they are considered and pursued is to switch the emphasis from individual innovations to a deeper and broader concern with innovativeness. It must become part of the fabric of the whole organization. Focusing on the major opportunities with a 'big project' mentality can be disastrous. It introduces a 'get it right first time' attitude, rather than an iterative, experimental approach. This rarely works:

■ *RCA and CBS had an early lead in the VCR market. They adopted an old style, 'dominate the market' approach, betting heavily on one big project. They had large teams of engineers working in isolated research laboratories.*

Sony and JVC were underfunded by comparison. Starting out from behind they proceeded slowly and with humility – testing, modifying and listening. They now dominate the market worldwide.

INNOVATIVENESS: PART OF THE COST OF BEING IN BUSINESS

Firms which focus on individual innovations make a very dangerous assumption. They typically evaluate each innovative idea or new venture on its own merits: how much will it cost? What are the risks? What are the returns? and so on. The assumption they are making is this: their base business – and the profits that it generates – will continue, irrespective of whether they innovate or not. This has been proved false time and again, in industry after industry. Innovation is not just a source of potentially attractive new opportunities, but an inescapable cost of staying in business. This will become increasingly true as the pace of change accelerates in markets worldwide.

Firms which do not accept this and do not take into account the cost of being innovative are merely deluding themselves. They may be able to report good profits in their accounts today, but if they are not innovative then these profits will be transitory. No industry or market is immune from change. Sooner or later fundamental changes will take place in the way in which the business operates. When this happens, innovative firms will prosper. Those which are not are unlikely to survive.

Peter Drucker* correctly identified profits as being not so much a reward for past performance, but rather one of the costs of staying in business. So it is with innovativeness. There is nothing optional about it. Management cannot feel free to choose whether the financial returns from innovation make the necessary investment worthwhile or not. Their core business simply must remain vital, able to adapt to the rapidly evolving environment. Being innovative should instead be thought of as an inescapable part of the firm's cost structure, just like raw materials or taxes. These costs are real: innovative organizations will spend more time investigating new ideas and critically questioning the

---

* *Peter F. Drucker*, Management in Turbulent Times.

way in which they run their business. They will spend time and money trying out new concepts, many of which will fail. They will continuously be experimenting and pushing back the frontiers of their understanding of their business. All of this costs money. In the short term, this expense could be avoided. But it is a dangerous false economy, like avoiding the costs of training, quality control or advertising. It can boost earnings today, but often at the cost of performance or even survival tomorrow. Profit without innovation is illusory. It cannot continue indefinitely.

Unlike many other important parts of the firm's cost structure, however, the cost of being innovative is hidden. There is no line in the profit and loss account labelled 'innovation'. (The costs of the research and development function are, of course, only one aspect of the overall investment in innovation. Much of research and development has relatively little to do with business innovation. Conversely, many fundamental innovations do not rely upon any technical advances or research.) The costs of innovation are both actual costs and opportunity costs:

- Actual costs: include the management time and effort spent on developing new concepts and the cash costs of testing and exploiting them.

- Opportunity costs: can often be even more significant than the actual costs. Time and effort spent on innovation is time which could have been employed in other profitable ways: in improving the operating efficiency of today's business; in generating additional sales and profits. These lost or deferred opportunities are part of the real cost of innovation.

MEASURING THE PROCESS: THE INNOVATIVENESS AUDIT

Innovativeness, then, is a critical aspect of management approach and performance, so we need to be able to control and measure it. How innovative are we today? How much are we investing in innovativeness? Should it be more? Less? Should we be doing it in different ways? There are, of course, no hard and fast answers, no concrete rules. We are dealing with strategic questions of the future direction of the firm. Numerous factors must come into play: the industry within which the firm operates, its current competitive position in that industry, actual and likely developments among customers and suppliers, changes in the regulatory environment, technological developments, competitors' initiatives and so on. Most of all, it rests upon management's beliefs and judgement. What do they see as the opportunities and threats over the medium and long term?

Without being able to measure accurately either current investment in innovation or performance in it, managements are in a vacuum when making decisions on what changes to make. Worse still, in many companies these decisions are never explicitly taken. Innovations occur or do not occur in a haphazard way. Management have effectively abdicated control over this key aspect of their strategy. The famous physicist, Lord Kelvin, once observed that until one was able to measure something, one's true knowledge of what is going on is severely limited. This holds true in business. We have to be able to measure innovativeness. The **innovativeness audit** can be a powerful tool to help make better strategic decisions. It will not in itself provide concrete prescriptions. What it can do, however, is to provide management with insight and information. It raises the level of debate. It makes innovativeness explicit.

In essence an innovativeness audit is quite straightforward. It involves an explicit and comprehensive review of all relevant aspects of the firm's innovativeness. By ensuring that all these factors are considered, it enables management to base decisions and actions on the fullest possible information. The key elements of it are:

- **How much** are we investing in innovation?
- **Which areas** are we investing in?
- Who is **leading the effort?**
- Do we generate **sufficient innovative ideas?**
- When we evaluate them, do we **accept too many? Too few?**
- How well do we **implement innovation?**

Getting innovation right is not easy. It requires good decisions and effective actions at each stage. Failure in any one stage can jeopardize the whole process. The audit measures the company's performance. It helps to pinpoint where the firm is doing well, and where it needs to change. The precise questions to ask and analyses to perform vary for each individual company. A good place to start is:

- **Investment:** how much management time is devoted to innovation? In particular, how much consideration is given to new ideas and approaches within the normal planning and reporting cycles of the business? In some companies regular management meetings are given over entirely to discussing day-to-day concerns, with no priority at all given to innovation. In others there is always a significant portion of such meetings which is devoted to considering new approaches to various aspects of the business. Some have regular working sessions where innovation is the sole item on the agenda. Once the management time involved is identified, it is possible to estimate the equivalent level of investment which is being made. Can we discover anything about our competitors: how much do they invest?

- **Idea generation:** over the course of two or three years, how many new ideas have been considered and evaluated? It is useful to measure this as an indication of whether a sufficient flow of new opportunities is being generated. Beyond a simple count of the number of ideas generated, it can be extremely revealing to split them up into different categories: new products or services, changes to the manufacturing process, new distribution methods, tailoring the offering for particular groups of customers and so on. This will often reveal that the majority of innovative ideas considered have been of one particular type, with far fewer ideas elsewhere. (Typically, product or service innovation ideas will be most common, with far less emphasis being given to other aspects of the business system. Occasionally, such an approach is entirely appropriate. More often, however, it suggests that there are lost opportunities elsewhere.)

- **Participation:** from where in the organization are the firm's innovative ideas coming? Analysing the ideas which have been considered in the last two or three years can show which areas and levels of the organization are generating the ideas. The pattern which emerges can point strongly to improvements need to be made. Two pronounced patterns often emerge:

  - In many companies most of the new ideas are being generated quite high up in the organization. Opportunities are being missed: the creative energies and insights of junior and middle management are not being fully exploited.

  - Often it is the marketing department which comes up with most of the ideas. Their efforts are indeed laudable, but opportunities which exist in other areas of the business are probably being passed by.

- **The process:** it is useful to lay out the mechanisms by which individual managers can communicate and push their innovative ideas. In some companies there are quite clear forums in which this is encouraged to take place. In others, the way the organization works seems to make innovation difficult, even actively to discourage it. Such organizations innovate in spite of themselves – if at all. A specific question to consider is that of how the normal career path accommodates managers who may wish to push and exploit new ideas. Often it simply does not, in which case the company's innovative performance will be severely hampered.

- **Implementing innovation:** how successfully has the firm implemented innovations in the past? A list should be drawn up of all the innovations which the company has pursued in the past, say, five years. What proportion have been successes? What has been the return on the firm's investment – both in absolute terms and relative to the firm's expectations? What impact has innovation had on the company's existing core business – has it taken the company in the directions it wanted to move? Has the firm been more successful with some kinds of innovation than with others? In those instances where innovative attempts have been unsuccessful, what were the reasons? Poor evaluation? Slow decision-making? Over- or under-resourcing? Innovations can succeed or fail for a wide variety of reasons. Properly analysed, past performance can provide a rich source of information and valuable pointers for where the firm can make improvements.

- **Culture and beliefs:** these lie at the heart of how the whole organization functions. If innovation is not seen by most managers as a central part of their responsibilities, then the firm will be a poor creator of new opportunities. Identifying the beliefs of managers in various parts of the organization and what they consider to be their responsibilities is critical to understanding the basic forces which are driving the company. This requires a programme of in-depth one-on-one interviews with a representative sample of managers to determine their views of their own jobs and responsibilities, as well as their vision of the firm and the strategic challenges which face it. An important part of this is to identify what they consider to be the key success factors which will determine the company's performance over the medium to long term. Does innovation play a major role? In addition to the one-on-one interviews, group discussion sessions can sometimes be very fruitful in generating ideas and raising a lot of the issues which might otherwise go undiscovered. (Chapter 13, Innovation and Conceptual Maps, covers this important topic in greater depth.)

- **The industry track record:** over a period of several years all the significant successful innovations in the industry should be written down. For each one a note should be made of whether the firm was a/the leader in the industry, whether it followed others quickly or was late in adopting the new ideas. The innovations can be characterized by type as in the earlier section. Together, these analyses should give a clear idea of whether the firm is a leader or a follower and whether the whole industry's innovative efforts are balanced across several areas or focused on only a few. This may highlight fertile areas for investigation.

Taken together, the answers to these questions can begin to provide management with a clearer picture of how innovative their company is. The review can also provide the basic information they need to start prescribing changes to be made:

- Are we innovating in the right areas? Are there whole fields of opportunity which we may be missing?

- Is our culture supportive of innovation, or a barrier to it?

- Which parts of the organization do we have to focus on to become more innovative?

- What changes might be worth making to personnel evaluation and career structures? To the mechanisms by which new ideas are solicited and pursued?

- Are we spending enough on innovation? Do we invest too much?

Innovativeness in the broadest sense is becoming an increasingly important success factor in many businesses. The future belongs to those firms which succeed in understanding and managing the process of innovation. The innovativeness audit is one important tool in this process.

SUMMARY

Innovativeness is rapidly becoming an increasingly important source of competitive advantage for companies in all industries.

- As the **pace of change** quickens, management itself constitutes the most enduring and significant competitive advantage which a firm can have.

Innovativeness goes beyond actual **innovations.**

- It is a fundamental aspect of the way in which the firm approaches everything it does.

Companies can **manage for innovativeness.**

- An **audit** of the firm's innovative performance is the first step in providing the inputs and insight to manage this process.

13 INNOVATION AND CONCEPTUAL MAPS

All companies operate with a conceptual map (or intellectual framework) describing how their industry works. These maps are powerful. They determine every action the company makes.

Success breeds strong conceptual maps. If the map becomes too strong it acts as a barrier against change and innovation. Few companies actively manage their maps. It can be done. It is worthwhile.

13 INNOVATION AND CONCEPTUAL MAPS

- Competition in the mind

- The power of perceptions

- The map as a barrier to change

- Changing the map

COMPETITION IN THE MIND

Bruce Henderson, founder of the Boston Consulting Group, once stated that most competitive battles are won in the minds of the managers involved, not in the marketplace. There is a great deal of truth in this statement:

- If competition is head-on and cut-throat, all firms in the industry bleed. True, those with the strongest competitive position may suffer least – but no one gains from the bloodletting. Few industries continue with such competition for long. An approximate competitive equilibrium re-emerges with each player operating within a certain set of implicitly prescribed limits. Pursuing competition to its ultimate conclusion – the elimination of one's major competitors – is simply far too damaging and expensive for all concerned.

- Winning competitive wars of attrition is like fighting a battle in the trenches: muddy, bloody and rarely conclusive. The most profitable victories are those where one's competitor concedes defeat - or rather, concedes the re-establishment of the competitive equilibrium at a more favourable position – without an expensive battle.

  - *IBM appears to have a policy of announcing new models and standards well in advance of their introduction. Such is the company's strength in its market that these announcements serve to 'freeze' the standards in the way which best suits IBM. IBM's decisions set the industry norms.*

■ *In many industries a 'phoney war' can develop in which competitors successively announce new capacity additions before a single foundation stone is laid. Each is trying to pre-empt and discourage the others' plans. If all the mooted plants were to be built, there would be massive over-capacity in the industry. As soon as construction actually starts on one plant, many of the competitors' plans evaporate.*

■ *In his excellent book* The Other Guy Blinked, *Roger Enrico describes the Cola Wars fought between Pepsi and Coca Cola. Each tries to influence the other's behaviour by exploiting any real or perceived weaknesses in the market. Pepsi had heard in advance that Coca Cola was about to change the formula of its core product, Coke. Coca Cola would claim New Coke to be a major coup, a significant improvement on what was already the dominant product in the market. Pepsi stole the initiative by announcing the change ahead of the launch, claiming that it was Coca Cola's desperate response to the steady encroachments which Pepsi had been making on Coke's market share. It announced a day's holiday for all Pepsi employees to celebrate the victory. It followed this with an aggressive advertising campaign which played upon the disappointment which committed Coke drinkers were experiencing at the removal of the old product.*

Coca Cola were on the defensive. New Coke was not the success they had been hoping for. They eventually relaunched their old formula under the name Classic Coke. The combined market share of New and Classic Coke was below that of the original product before the change, and they had to cope with all the added complexity and cost of two major brands rather than one.

We will never know for sure how New Coke would have fared without Pepsi's intervention. One thing is certain: Pepsi's actions put Coca Cola on the defensive from the start. Coca Cola's perception of their products and the challenges they faced in the market cannot have failed to be influenced by Pepsi's campaign.

THE POWER OF PERCEPTIONS

The perceptions which we have of our business make up a **conceptual map** which is essential to analysis, inference and strategic management. Without such a framework, observations would become a mass of haphazard and meaningless data, rather than true information; managing a business would be rather like learning a foreign language with no rules of grammar or structure: a mass of data would have to be learned by rote; inference would be impossible.

Managers within a company normally share a conceptual map of their business and its environment. The stronger the firm and its culture, the more powerful this common vision tends to be. Organizations in which a common map does not exist find it difficult to operate effectively. Visions drive action. Conflicting visions lead to conflicting actions. Ultimately this destroys all coherence and momentum. The firm flounders, unable to generate the commitment it needs to move in one direction for long enough to get anywhere. Having said that, it is extremely healthy to have a certain disparity of vision within the firm. Without it, management can easily become stale, and innovation stifled.

Conceptual maps are an extremely powerful influence on our behaviour as managers. They can also be dangerous. The observations which we make and information we gather do not reflect reality so much as our filtered version of it. Our conceptual map determines:

- What information we perceive to be important and what we believe to be irrelevant or trivial.

- What information we collect in our management reporting, accounting and market research.

- How we analyse the information which we have collected.

- How we interpret the results of that analysis.

- How and to whom in the organization we communicate our interpretations.

THE MAP AS A BARRIER TO CHANGE

The danger is this: the more successful we are as individuals and firms, the more engrained our conceptual maps tend to become. Every success, however small, provides positive feedback which reinforces the map. The map in turn reinforces the corporate culture: successful firms tend to have strong cultures – or is it vice versa? When we receive information which conflicts with our map, the first reaction can be to rationalize it away, assume it is a fluke, or just plain ignore it. The strength of conceptual maps has profound implications for innovation:

- Successful firms with strong conceptual maps and corporate cultures can find fundamental innovation extremely difficult. For it requires that they cast aside the map which has served them so well in the past, and step into the unknown. The map can all too easily change from being a guide to become a straightjacket: information which is at odds with the map – and which might hold the seeds of innovative opportunities – is rejected. The innovative opportunities are discarded along with the information (Figure 27).

Figure 27: The initial conceptual map is reinforced by success and positive feedback. If it becomes too strong it can lead to conflicting information – and with it insights and opportunities – being rejected and lost.

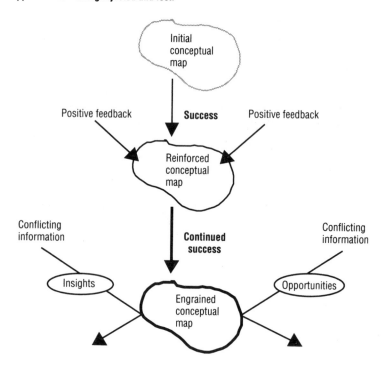

- *Henry Ford described the power and danger of strong conceptual maps in his 1922 book,* My Life and Work: *'Businessmen go down with their businesses because they like the old way so well they cannot bring themselves to change . . . Seldom does the cobbler take up with a new*

fangled way of soling shoes and seldom does the artisan willingly take up with the new methods in his trade.'

- *The innovator's greatest asset is often the strength of the entrenched competitor's maps. The more fundamentally new the concept is, the more likely it is to be rejected or ignored by the competitor – until it is too late. It is a constant source of amazement to innovators that their more established competitors allow them to grow for so long before reacting. It is very rare to see rapid and effective retaliation to strategic innovations. This slowness in response provides the innovator with all the window of opportunity he needs:*

  - *Emery failed to react swiftly enough to Federal Express. By the time it did respond, Federal had established an almost impregnable position in overnight courier services.*

  - *In the late 1960s and early 1970s NCR could see computer technology emerging rapidly. It even entered the computer business itself, but steadfastly left its traditional cash register business tied to electromechanical technology. It either did not see or refused to see the impact which computer technology would have on the cash register business. In 1971 a tiny competitor, DTS, brought out the first electronic cash register. In 1972 10 per cent of cash registers sold in the US were electronic. Four years later 90 per cent were.*

    NCR was forced to write off huge amounts of electromechanical product, and laid off some 20,000 staff. Its share price plummeted. The company's strong market share helped it to regain some lost ground – at great cost and hardship, however. The inevitable transition to the new technology would have been much more successful and far less traumatic had early and decisive action been taken. The strength of NCR's conceptual map prevented this from happening.

CHANGING THE MAP

Managing and changing conceptual maps is probably the most fundamental challenge which innovative firms face. New maps are needed to develop new insights and opportunities – yet continued success in the existing business requires that the established map should remain intact. The established map in most firms is remarkably resilient but the perceptions and attitudes it represents have to be challenged and destroyed where necessary. A new map has to be built, tested and revised until it works. Only then can new insights be generated. Only then can true strategic innovation take place.

It may be an external crisis which forces the company to admit that its conceptual map has become quite inadequate as a management tool. If so, the widespread recognition of the need for a new vision makes it relatively easy to change the map. (Having said which, it is amazing how long people can cling to maps which have clearly exceeded their useful lives.) If this stage is reached, however, the firm is likely to be in dire straits, to have lost contol. At this point a new vision is needed just to keep the company intact, never mind helping it to innovate.

The ideal time at which to develop a new conceptual map is when the company is doing well. At this point managers have the luxury of experimenting with various new ideas until they reach a new vision which will take them on to further growth and success. Changing maps is always difficult, but less so if it can be done in a relaxed and ordered manner. Waiting until the existing map has failed limits the firm's options to act boldly and creatively. It forces an ad hoc approach on the firm. It limits the potential scope of the strategic vision.

The behaviour of animals can teach us something in this regard. In a standard experiment, two rats are placed in identical mazes with an identical cache of food at the end. They are made familiar with the maze through several repetitions of the experiment. One of the rats is then starved for a long period, while the other is fed normally. They are both put into their mazes once more. This time, however, a short-cut has been introduced. The result is always the same: the starved rat heads off down the familiar path at high speed, but is always beaten to the food by the well fed rat which takes the time to explore what lies down the new route. The influence is clear: it is difficult to be innovative when you are against the ropes.

Although the best time to develop a new conceptual map is when things are going well for the firm, this is also clearly in some senses the most difficult time. The firm's success is confirmation of the adequacy of the map. Why change? Developing a new vision at this time requires conscious and proactive management effort. There are a number of actions which can be taken:

- **Challenging the existing map:** is the most direct action which management can take. It involves two stages: first defining the map, and then testing it. Conceptual maps are rarely laid out in black and white – and extremely seldom in sufficient detail to reflect the full flavour and subtleties of what goes on within the firm. To be at all useful, the map has to be defined to a considerable level of detail: What business are we really in? What does the customer really buy? Which customers? What do we provide that is different from our competitors? How can one generate a competitive advantage in this business? Do we have a competitive advantage? And so on. The map is supposed to help explain what makes the organization function – so one must understand the visions and motivations of people in different roles at all levels in the firm.

This requires an objective assessment to be made of how individuals see their own and the firm's role and mission. In some firms this process can be conducted internally, while in others achieving the required objectivity requires bringing in outsiders to conduct the review. The best route depends upon the firm's structure and management resources: are there individuals available who are far enough removed from day-to-day operations to conduct the objective review which is required?

The outcome of this review should be a concise but comprehensive statement of the firm's current conceptual map and strategy. To be useful it must be both clear and testable: vague generalities are of relatively little use. The clearer and more precise it is, the easier it will be to complete the process: testing the map. In principle this involves nothing more that challenging every hypothesis and statement in the map. Sometimes this may need specially commissioned market research and analysis. More often a careful examination of how the map accords with observed reality is sufficient. The critical input is always an open, objective and questioning frame of mind. There should be no avenue left unexplored, no holy cows. At the end of the process most parts of the map will probably have withstood the examination and be left intact – all the stronger for having been tested. Some hypotheses and assumptions will, however, have been found to be invalid. Replacing these with an alternative, more correct set of hypotheses is the most creative and vital stage of the process: it is this which builds the new vision. Through this are created the new opportunities.

How frequently should the map be reviewed? Not often: if the review becomes part of an annual planning cycle it is almost bound to be relegated to an almost meaningless form-filling exercise. That situation is far worse than not reviewing the map at all: management only deceive themselves by thinking that their map is still valid when in fact it may not be, and has not even been tested. It should be done properly every five years or so – unless it is evident before then that some major change in the industry requires that it be done sooner.

- **Unexplained successes and failures:** are opportunities in disguise. They crop up from time to time in all businesses. They are never haphazard. There is an explanation for everything. If the existing conceptual map cannot explain why something has occurred, then it needs revision somewhere. This provides a valuable opportunity for management to test the validity of their conceptual map: whenever some unexplained phenomenon occurs they should investigate until it is fully understood. Quite often some seemingly minor event can signal the need for major changes to the map. Analysing unexplained events can provide a valuable early warning system – one which too few companies fully exploit. (For a further discussion of unexplained successes and failures see Chapter 4: Looking for Innovation.)

- **Organizational initiatives:** the culture within most firms is inextricably linked with their conceptual maps. The stronger the culture, the more difficult it is to change the map. Successful organizations operate like status quo machines. The more successful they are the stronger the barriers to change tend to be. These barriers cannot – indeed should not – be completely removed. The self-perpetuating ability of the successful firm is one of its greatest strengths. What must be done is to ensure that the barriers are not so strong as to make the organization incapable of changing.

For the most part this simply requires adopting a commonsense approach. Firstly, how open is the organization to external influences? What proportion of its activities are conducted with the outside world, and what proportion are purely internal? A steady flow of external information, ideas and perspectives is the raw material required to start producing insights. Far too many large organizations cut themselves off from this flow, thereby losing opportunities (broadcasting in Europe, for example, has suffered from this problem). Secondly, how is the firm organized? In large units or small ones? Along customer dimensions or in terms of internal criteria? The larger and more internally-oriented are the organizational units, the greater the problems: vested interests become more vociferous and powerful.

Sometimes, reducing the barriers is insufficient by itself: some more direct initiative is required. Some companies have tried setting up small groups of people working on projects outside the main body of the organization. They can find it much easier to challenge the existing map. Their success is usually greatest where there is some specific, finite task to be achieved (such as the development of IBM's PC.) The main problem with using this approach, however, is that of integrating the new vision back into the mainstream of the organization. The common result is that the individual innovations are not translated into a broader innovativeness: if this happens, the initiative has failed to resolve the fundamental problem. The key management challenge is to use these independent groups ('skunk works') as the thin end of the wedge to change the conceptual map of the parent organization itself.

The conceptual map is one of the most nebulous notions in business – and one of the most powerful. It is the soul of the firm. All actions and initiatives emanate from it. The map determines how innovative the firm will be, and in which directions it will head.

Conceptual maps can be defined and tested. Once this is done, they can be managed and revised where needed. Few firms do this explicitly. Most allow their maps to evolve and develop naturally. Often this results in an even more entrenched vision building up – until it fails cataclysmically. Then the need for a new map is clear. But it is extraordinarily risky and difficult to wait until then to change the map. Firms which do this are missing out on one of the greatest inputs they can make to their innovative performance. Manage the map.

SUMMARY

Managers' perceptions are the fundamental driving force behind company performance.

- The **conceptual map** summarizes the vision shared within the firm of its environment, business and strategy.

A strong and coherent map is needed to build commitment to a strategy and to deliver good performance.

- Yet, the stronger the conceptual map, the more difficult it is to change it – and the more difficult innovation becomes.

Strategic innovation requires changing conceptual maps.

- Constructively **challenging the existing map**
- Exploiting **unexplained successes and failures**
- **Taking organizational initiatives** to develop a new map.

14 ADAPTIVE AND REPETITIVE BEHAVIOUR

Companies display characteristic patterns of behaviour. Some are predominantly adaptive, others are repetitive.

Success requires a balance. If either side becomes too strong the firm's performance begins to suffer.

Attaining the balanced position is not easy: it is an unstable equilibrium. Few firms achieve it. It has to be consciously managed. Undertaking a behavioural review is the first stage in actively managing the company's behavioural patterns.

14 ADAPTIVE AND REPETITIVE BEHAVIOUR

- From innovation to cash generation

- Managing transitions and diversity

- Patterns of behaviour

- Achieving a balance

- Birth and growth
  - Excessive adaptation

- Consolidation and maturity
  - Excessive repetition

- Evolution and the unstable equilibrium

- Managing the balance
  - The behavioural review

FROM INNOVATION TO CASH GENERATION

Innovation is one of the most important challenges facing business today. Competitive pressures increasingly demand that companies adopt an innovative approach to all aspects of their operations. Without this, stagnation results. The unchanging goal of all companies, however, is to maintain a high and continuously improving financial performance. To achieve this, innovation in a narrow sense is insufficient. Generating and developing attractive new concepts is not enough in itself. Innovation must be integrated into the overall functioning of the firm and viewed in the context of the whole organization: its strategy, style and cash flow.

Promising ideas have to be converted into secure competitive positions and prolific generators of cash. Otherwise they merely consume resources. Without this there can be no dividends for the shareholders, no future for the firm. And no more innovation.

There are three basic stages which the firm must go through in achieving its goal: acquiring an adaptive approach, choosing a strategic direction and exploiting its repetitive skills.

- It must be **adaptive** in its approach, in order to generate innovative opportunities. Following the tried and tested approaches it knows is not enough. Clinging to past successes to the exclusion of new ideas is a guarantee of eventual failure. Businesses have to detach themselves from the past before they can embrace the future. Many once great companies have failed to do this and suffered as a result.

  - *Volkswagen's Beetle was such a success story that by the early 1970s the firm had become virtually a one product company. Beetles were produced with marvellous efficiency, as every operation had been honed down to a fine art, every opportunity for cost reduction exploited to the full.*

    In the process, the firm had lost its adaptive skills: it had not developed any significant new products for years, and had almost forgotten how to do so. The newer, more attractive offerings of its competitors were increasingly gaining ground on the Beetle, threatening the company's very survival.

    Volkswagen adapted just in time, coming up with the new Golf, which went on to give the firm even greater success. It was, however, a close-run thing.

- Having developed an adaptive approach and generated a range of innovative opportunities, the firm must choose a **strategic direction**. The more adaptive the firm is, the more difficult this can be: there will be numerous potentially attractive opportunities. The company must choose between them. They cannot all be pursued, for to do so would dissipate resources and destroy the firm's momentum. Failure to make a coherent choice rarely goes unpunished for long:

  - *Several of the conglomerates formed in the 1960s lacked a truly coherent strategic direction. Their generally poor long-term performance reflects this. More recently, the trend among many of them has been to divest themselves of their non-core activities to regain a sense of focus.*

  - *One large Scandinavian natural resource business was a strong generator of cash, but with limited growth prospects. It had a strong need to diversify, but lacked a clear vision of where it should be heading. Undeterred, it started buying up companies. Management acquired several businesses in a wide diversity of areas, hoping to hedge its bets. The resulting unmanageable portfolio of businesses performed predictably poorly. A new management team disposed of many of them, refocusing the firm on a smaller number of core areas.*

- ■ Innumerable innovative young companies fail because they pursue too many attractive opportunities simultaneously. They simply stretch themselves too thinly.

● Having decided upon a strategic direction, the firm must **focus** carefully, exploiting its **repetitive** skills to learn by experience. It must manage its costs downwards and progressively refine its offering to its customers. It is only by doing this that its innovative ideas can be turned into major cash generators.

MANAGING TRANSITIONS AND DIVERSITY

These stages require different and conflicting patterns of behaviour:

● **Adaptive** behaviour is required to generate new ideas to replace previously held visions and conceptual maps. Mould-breaking and creativity are called for.

● **Repetitive** behaviour is then needed to build an experience base and progressively refine the firm's concepts and operations. Focus and attention to detail are of paramount importance.

These different behaviour patterns do not sit together easily. Each requires specific management skills:

● **Transition management:** the single-product or single-business company needs to foster particular behaviour traits in the early stages of development and then to discard these in favour of different traits later on. Transition management is an important determinant of success.

- ■ It is for this reason the original entrepreneurs in a business only rarely remain with it until the firm reaches maturity. Different basic behaviour patterns are required. The very skills that make someone a gifted creator and entrepreneur are often at odds with the needs of the maturing firm.

- **Diversity management:** in multi-product or multi-business companies there will at any one time be individual businesses at different stages of their development. These businesses will have diametrically opposed behavioural needs. Success in some will require highly adaptive behaviour, while others need repetitive skills to perform well. Diversity management is needed to enable these skills to co-exist.

  - Many mature firms find that the only sure way to foster the adaptive skills they need is to set up organizationally independent 'skunk works'. They find it very difficult to have adaptive and repetitive patterns flourishing within the one organization.

  - Most traditional conglomerates are managed via tight financial reporting and controls. These tend to favour repetitive behaviour at the expense of adaptation. It is difficult to support creativity in an organization where all attention is focused on the next quarter's profit and cash flow. As a result, few conglomerates are innovative.

PATTERNS OF BEHAVIOUR

Achieving the right balance between different behavioural patterns and successfully making transitions between them is an important factor in generating superior corporate performance. These behavioural patterns are not arbitrary. They are a direct result of the firm's environment, strategy and management approach. They can be influenced. The first stage in controlling these behavioural patterns is to understand them in greater depth. It is only then that prescriptive action can be defined.

Companies are groups of individuals, bonded together with a common vision or conceptual map. The best place to start to understand behavioural traits at a company level is to examine individual behaviour. Most of us know people who fit one or other of the stereotypes:

- **Adaptive:** the person who is always trying out new ideas, continually experimenting; great on the big picture, less good on the detail of any particular situation. While the repetitive type views life with a telephoto lens, the adaptor has a wide angle: everything is included, but not in the same detail. Structure or tightly defined tasks and expectations limit and frustrate this person; he needs freedom to find his role and to see what can be made of it. Many of his new ideas fall flat. Some succeed spectacularly. Many more have the makings of great success, but fail for want of sufficient attention to detail. Tremendous spurts of energy in one direction can be followed by total neglect when a new challenge appears elsewhere. Something of a rebel and a loner, he works best in a loose, unstructured environment.

• **Repetitive:** the plodder, the person who learns by experience. A perfectionist at heart, this character takes pride in progressively improving his performance, quality and efficiency in a given role. Happiest in a well structured environment where tasks, responsibilities and expectations are clearly defined, he pays great attention to detail. Reliability is a particularly strong trait, compensating perhaps for a lack of imagination. His great strength is focus and stamina. Often a team player, he fits into existing structures and conforms with his peers.

These stereotypes are extremes: in reality we all have traces of both types in our make-up. The most balanced individuals have a fair measure of each: creativity tempered with practicality and perseverance. So it is with companies. The manifestations are very similar.

• **Adaptive (innovative):** firms which are forever developing new ideas, or adapting existing ones in novel ways to suit new markets. From a market and an organizational viewpoint they seem to be in a state of constant flux. No sooner has a new product been thoroughly debugged and tested in the market than a new range is introduced or the company moves off to tackle new opportunities. Despite all the hustle and bustle, however, the company never really seems to arrive anywhere. While its profits may seem good, its cash flow often appears only sufficient to fund new developments, with little left over for the shareholders.

• **Repetitive (efficient):** firms with a clear focus and strong position in either one or a small number of market segments. Its products or services meet its customers' needs well, and are typically superior to those of its competitors. The company seems to be supremely good at those things which it focuses on. Its products are extremely well and efficiently made. Sometimes it seems immune to its competitors' attacks. Although it is a steady performer, however, the company is going nowhere fast. New products are rare. The company sticks to what it knows best. Although profits and cash flow seem excellent, there is a risk: if the market – or the customers, technology or competitors – change rapidly, it can appear leaden-footed. Having focused so long and so hard on one area, it finds it difficult to break out of its established pattern when it needs to.

ACHIEVING A BALANCE

Of course, no company is exclusively adaptive or exclusively repetitive in character, but most are predominantly one or the other. This chapter will show how the most successful companies – like the most successful individuals – achieve a balance between the two, drawing upon the strengths of each type (Figure 28.) In today's fast-moving business environment, the term 'repetition' is often used in a pejorative way, indicating conservatism, lack of imagination and boredom, all of which are anathema to today's executive who values change, creativity and progress. Indeed, taken to the extreme, repetition is dangerous. Yet without it, nothing would be possible. There would be no economies of scale, no cost reductions through experience. Products would never become perfected, and companies would never generate sufficient cash flows to fund new product developments. Innovations would remain nothing more than bright ideas, consuming cash rather than producing it. In short, economic progress itself would be impossible. It is a matter of balance.

Now let's consider what happens to an innovative firm as it goes through the phases of its development. It is important to focus here on truly innovative young firms, the mould breakers. Firms which provide some standard product or service that fits into the existing pattern of their industry do not concern us here. They have fundamentally different behaviour patterns. Not surprisingly, the mix between adaptive and repetitive behaviour varies as the firm evolves.

BIRTH AND GROWTH

The innovative young firm sets out with a particular culture and behavioural style. These evolve rapidly as it progresses, and the firm

Figure 28: Successful companies achieve a balance between adaptive and repetitive behaviour

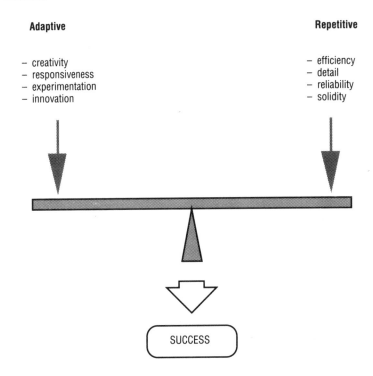

Adaptive

- creativity
- responsiveness
- experimentation
- innovation

Repetitive

- efficiency
- detail
- reliability
- solidity

SUCCESS

soon develops its own distinctive patterns. Three factors have a particular influence on the company's emerging style.

- **Fundamental approach:** if it is ever going to be a truly significant competitor in its industry, a firm must have genuinely new and mould-breaking ideas. Otherwise it is merely yet another supplier of the same product or service. True innovation requires that the firm should look at its market, its product, its customers, indeed its whole business system in a new way. Accepted truths have to be questioned, lest they become straightjackets. In other words, the fundamental approach of the innovative company is adaptive in nature. It sets off with a new conceptual map.

- **People:** it takes a certain type of individual to start a new firm, to embark upon a significantly innovative venture. Innovators are non-conformist by nature. Further, the original impetus to start a new venture is often a desire to break out of an existing structure and find a new, more fluid and immediate environment in which to operate. Somewhat surprisingly, this seems to be almost as powerful a driver of innovative behaviour as the desire to make money per se.

■ *Ron Lander, Chairman of Scetlander, a highly innovative Glasgow-based educational software publisher, recollects: 'Our family had sold Lander Alarms to the RMC Group in December 1979. I stayed with the Group, taking the Lander Alarms business from number eight to around number three nationally. However, I have always disliked structure and bureaucracies – even those of my own making. So in 1985, despite the excellent prospects for the company and me, I left and set up Scotlander as a vehicle for further ventures. Scetlander is the first of these.'*

■ *Tom Farmer, founder and Chairman of Kwit-Fit, Europe's largest automotive parts retailer and the dominant force in the British tyre and exhaust market, recalls his reasons for leaving Brown Brothers & Albany, a company which he had helped build: 'The merger between my own company (Tyre & Accessory Supplies) and Albany in 1968 had gone well. I got on really well with Stenson and Knight, Albany's co-founders – we had a great relationship and could work together effectively. We were really close to the market and knew all our staff. In 1969 we took over Brown Brothers, a firm about six times our size. All of a sudden it was too large, and I stopped enjoying it so much. I decided to retire to the US. It didn't take long before I got bored. A year later I set up Kwik-Fit.'*

● **Feedback:** once the new firm starts to trade, it begins to get feedback from the market. If its innovation is really significant and valuable to customers, a familiar pattern often emerges. Word spreads about the new product or service, and potential customers from different markets begin to ask for it for a wide range of applications.

■ *Instachain of Sweden was a start-up firm which had developed an automatic snow chain for large trucks. It enabled the driver to deploy the chain at the flick of a switch, instead of having to handle several hundredweight of dirty chains in the ice and snow. Once it started showing its new chain at trade shows, the firm was soon inundated with enquiries from all directions: what about a model for passenger cars? For trucks between six and ten tonnes? For buses? For the particular needs of the American market? Flattered by this level of interest, and being technically-minded anyway, the management were only too pleased to oblige, and began development projects in a whole range of areas.*

- *After a promising period in the 1960s, rotary engines had fallen out of favour in the automotive world. Fuel consumption was poor and problems with cylinder seals limited engine lifetimes. Norton Motors continued developing their product. The firm became a lone voice in the wilderness, a missionary for rotary engines. They doggedly and consistently resolved the earlier problems with these engines and improved performance to the point where they rivalled (and for certain applications, surpassed) reciprocating engines. Ten years of effort had paid off. By the mid-1980s Norton's engine offered superb reliability and a superior power-to-weight ratio. Interest grew in the engine, and enquiries began to flow in from a wide range of potential users: aircraft companies, car manufacturers, generator companies, industrial users, outboard engine suppliers etc. Keen to continue development, and eager for the research contract revenues involved, Norton responded to these requests and pursued opportunities in a diverse range of areas.*

Instachain and Norton are typical of the innovative young company with a potentially major success on their hands. All the feedback they get and all their early experience in the market confirms the wide potential for the product. It reinforces the tendency in the firm to be adaptive. Every promising avenue is pursued, so that no opportunity is lost.

Taken together, these three factors – that is, the company's fundamental approach, the people involved and the feedback from the market – incline the firm strongly towards adaptive behaviour (Figure 29). Every natural instinct and influence drives the firm to be adaptive. The more successful the firm is, the stronger these tendencies become.

Figure 29: All influences on new and growing firms tend to support and accentuate adaptive behaviour.

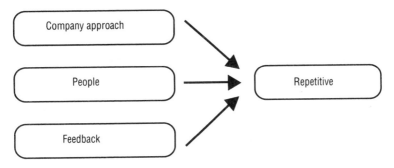

Excessive adaptation

Consider the implications of this (Figure 30). With such a strong tendency towards adaptation, the firm can easily lose all focus in its strategy and operations. 'Focus' is a great business virtue. It requires making sacrifices. It implies that the growing firm must concentrate on one or perhaps two areas of opportunity and leave the others until later. This is extremely difficult to do: that company from Canada which wants the engine for its portable generators just might be on to

Figure 30: An overly-adaptive approach in the growing firm can lead to a lack of focus and potential failure.

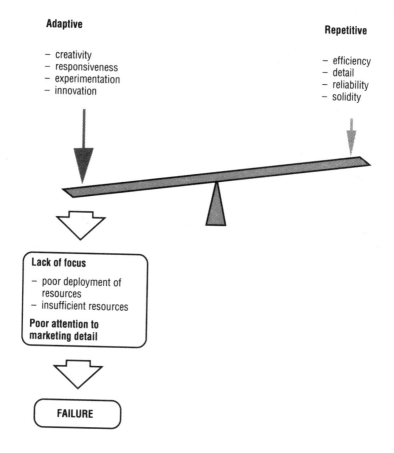

Adaptive

   – creativity
   – responsiveness
   – experimentation
   – innovation

Repetitive

   – efficiency
   – detail
   – reliability
   – solidity

Lack of focus

   – poor deployment of
     resources
   – insufficient resources

**Poor attention to
marketing detail**

FAILURE

something big. Think of the marginal revenue we could get from this potential user who wants some slight variant to try out in his products. So the firm pursues all or most of the opportunities. Then the inevitable happens. Scarce resources – people and capital – are stretched unbelievably thinly. With so many projects and leads proceeding in tandem, there is a feeling of great activity and accomplishment. However, this is deceptive: progress in individual areas is held back by the insufficient resources deployed in each one. Frequent changes of direction prevent any momentum from being built up. The administrative complexity of controlling so many areas grows exponentially and can soon swamp the firm: it loses control.

■ *Both Norton and Instachain fell victim to this disease – in large part because of the very strength of their products. Happily, both now have new managements who have refocused on their core strengths.*

■ *These problems are not new. Riley had a strong reputation in the 1920s and 1930s for high performance lightweight cars. They won at Le Mans several times. The firm had a devoted following of enthusiasts who would frequently ask for special versions, modifications and new models. Riley was only too happy to oblige. It ended up with an extremely wide product range. In 1936 a Riley advertisement stated: '. . . we make far too many models, of course. But then, we have a pretty fertile design department and we like making nice, interesting cars.' In 1937 the firm moved into a loss-making position. In 1938 it was taken over by Nuffield.*

There is another, sadly widespread, mistake made; this leads managements almost to abdicate marketing and strategic responsibility. The seductive reasoning runs like this: We have developed a great new product: look at all the people who want to try one out in their own applications. This requires that we focus on the technical development: after all that's what we are best at. Marketing and strategy will have to wait: our customers know their own markets far better than we ever will, and they assure us that they can use thousands once they have completed testing and we have solved the bearing fatigue/shelf life/costing/etc problem. So the firm concentrates all its efforts on this one aspect of the business. It ignores – temporarily, of course – other equally vital areas. The implications are obvious: with only a patchy understanding of the market, the company is unable to determine in which direction it should move, and where its development efforts (technical and marketing) should be focused. Management are too busy responding to the day-to-day needs arising from all the leads they are pursuing. In short, they cannot set a logical strategy. Instead of charting its own course, the firm loses control. It is tossed around by every force and reaction in the market.

This natural tendency to adaptation claims many casualties. Highly promising innovative firms become victims of their own success. More truly promising young companies fail for these reasons than for the lack of a good and saleable idea. They simply grow too quickly – or, more correctly, they grow in too uncontrolled a manner.

CONSOLIDATION AND MATURITY

As the firm matures, its culture and behavioural style continue to evolve. It is influenced by the same factors as before, but these now pull it in a different direction.

- **Fundamental approach:** it is a frequently observed fact that most successful mature companies derive almost all their profit from one or two core businesses. These are the businesses where the company enjoys a particularly strong position relative to its competitors in that segment. They are in all senses the very core of the corporation. The mature company will typically have a number of other businesses and markets of differing size, growth and profitability. In aggregate, however, these other businesses are only rarely significant in comparison with the core. The corporation stands or falls on the performance of its core.

  Most companies know where their core is. The precise numbers may not be available, but management at all levels recognize where the real source of cash flow lies. They protect the core. While recognizing the future importance of innovation and new ventures, management – quite rightly – place the highest priority on the core. In the well run mature company every opportunity for improving its performance is pursued with vigour – cost reductions, rationalizations, ever more refined marketing segmentation. The key skill is learning from experience. Radical changes can entail unacceptable risks for uncertain rewards. Change is evolutionary rather than revolutionary in nature. Each added unit of volume brings new opportunities to fine-tune the product or service more precisely. Thus, the fundamental approach of the company becomes conservative and repetitive in nature. The firm protects and builds on the status quo.

- **People:** successful mature companies tend naturally to attract a particular type of person: those who value security and structure in their work environment. The skills which these companies require above all others are those needed to maintain and build upon the strengths of their core businesses. In many companies this implies adopting an almost 'engineered' approach to all aspects of the business: making continuous slow improvements to each area of operations, based upon a significant and growing base of experience. Others require a keen diplomatic sense, so that long-standing and often subtle understandings and arrangements in the industry are respected. These are clearly people with repetitive behaviour patterns – the steady performers, the gradualists. In many situations, the visionary or rebel can be positively dangerous: a radical new policy that is extremely well argued and supported can jeopardize years of painstaking progress. These organizations tend not only to be unattractive to adaptive types in the first place, but also to frustrate and eventually drive them out if they do join – as the examples above showed.

  It is quite rare for founding members of a firm to stay with the business as it grows to maturity. Most entrepreneurs leave somewhere along the way as the business evolves through its different development phases. However, when they do stay, they represent a valuable asset for the business: a senior management which, almost by definition, has a blend of repetitive and adaptive skills.

- **Feedback:** the mature and successful firm receives strong feedback from its customers and the market in general. Its very size and success are due to the way it has developed its core business over the years. The lessons it has learned along the way have become engrained in the corporate culture as firmly held truths. They constitute its conceptual map. In many businesses market shares will change only slowly over time. The key to success appears to be providing the customers with the high quality products or services they have grown accustomed to – and continuously but gradually making improvements to them.

  Investing in improvements to product quality, or cost reductions often has an excellent payback. Repetitive skills are rewarded. Conversely, the firm may well have made forays into new markets with innovative products, but only a small proportion of these will have been successful. Only rarely will attempts at innovation have shown a payback comparable to investments in the base business. The feedback which the company receives therefore tends to reinforce its behavioural traits, i.e. its repetitive skills.

In summary, we have exactly the opposite situation to the new growth firm. In the mature firm the fundamental approach and culture, the people and the feedback from the market all support and reinforce its **repetitive** behaviour patterns (Figure 31). Once again, the whole process is self-reinforcing: the more successful the company is in its core markets, the stronger are these fundamental tendencies reinforced.

Figure 31: All influences on consolidating and mature firms tend to support and accentuate repetitive behaviour.

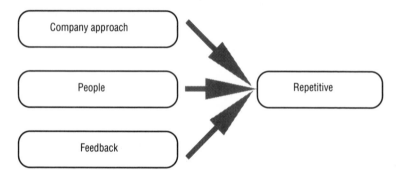

Excessive repetition

The dangers of too great an emphasis on repetitive behaviour will now be clear (Figure 32). Large and successful firms focus increasingly carefully on their core businesses. This is healthy and should continue. What can happen, however, is that they begin to do this within the confines of their existing conceptual map. Their experience has reinforced their view of how the industry and their customers behave. Over the years they have learned what are the key management variables in the business – market share, unit costs, margins per square foot, stock turn, run length or whatever. They track these increasingly carefully. Taken to extremes, this can be very dangerous. From being a reflection of the business realities, these measures become the reality. Instead of running a business, top management end up running a set of numbers.

The hard-won lessons of experience become a straightjacket; management produce programmed answers to each market situation. Creativity, responsiveness, even the ability to change can be lost.

Figure 32: An overly repetitive approach in the mature or consolidating firm can lead to stagnation, lack of responsiveness and potential failure.

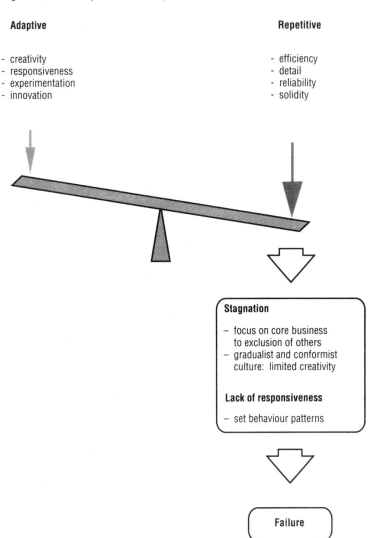

Adaptive

- creativity
- responsiveness
- experimentation
- innovation

Repetitive

- efficiency
- detail
- reliability
- solidity

Stagnation

– focus on core business
  to exclusion of others
– gradualist and conformist
  culture: limited creativity

Lack of responsiveness

– set behaviour patterns

Failure

What of innovation? This requires a questioning approach to the accepted truths of the industry. It requires rejecting existing conceptual maps. But if those with the skill and character to do this have long left the business, its ability – indeed its very desire – to innovate will be weak.

All of this need not matter too much – as long as the industry remains stable. The company can continue generating an excellent positive cash flow. It will typically pay healthy dividends to its shareholders and invest a lot (sometimes too much, especially in the later stages) in its core businesses. It may also invest – usually with less success – in diversifications and new ventures. Taken as a whole, however, its performance is pefectly adequate – if a little unexciting, perhaps.

And then something fundamental changes in the industry: a competitor's innovation, a new technology, emergence of new customer needs, a step-change in the economics of the industry, for example. How does the market leader respond? Often, not at all. The firm has become trapped by its conceptual map and its own success. The signals from the market are attributed to a temporary downturn, the dollar exchange rate, a product quality problem, a poor advertising campaign – anything, in fact, other than a fundamental sea-change in the whole industry and competitive environment. The map cannot be wrong. And so inappropriate actions are taken – often exacerbating the root cause of the problem. By the time the leader does make a fundamental reassessment of its business, it is often too late: the leadership position has been lost to the innovator.

Many managers in mature businesses will not believe this could happen in their industry. They will point out that the technology, the distribution channels, the customers and the competitors behave in predictable ways. Therefore, innovation is neither an opportunity nor a threat to them. That was the attitude in the US steel business – before foreign competition and mini-mills changed the economics and competitive equilibrium of the whole industry. It was also the attitude in the US airline business before deregulation and low cost competitors changed everything. Ocean transportation was a mature industry until Sea Land introduced the concept of containerization.

In reality, there is no industry where innovation does not have a role to play. The risk that the mature firm takes in becoming too set in its repetitive behaviour patterns is two-fold:

- **Missed opportunities:** it will fail to spot and exploit the innovative opportunities which exist in every industry.

- **Vulnerability:** it will fail to respond to fundamental changes and threats in the business. In so doing, it risks losing its dominant position.

EVOLUTION AND THE UNSTABLE EQUILIBRIUM

When the new growth firm and the mature market leader are looked at together, a clear pattern emerges: each runs the risk of falling victim to the very character traits which provide its greatest strengths. Figure 33 demonstrates the problem.

Figure 33: Typical evolution of behaviour patterns as a firm progresses from birth to maturity

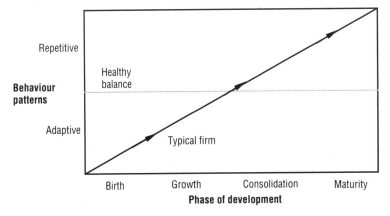

In any size or type of firm a balance is needed between adaptive and repetitive behaviour. Too much adaptation and the company will lose focus and, with it, momentum. Too much repetition and it will stagnate and, worse still, lose its ability to respond to changes in the environment. Both can be fatal. The natural tendency for the new firm is to be almost completely adaptive in nature. As the company develops it tends to become increasingly repetitive in nature. This is a frequently observed phenomenon. The early challenge is therefore to instil focus and control into the new venture. Without this the firm may be highly innovative yet fail to exploit its opportunities. As time progresses this becomes less of an issue. The key requirement later on is just the opposite: to inject some excitement and creativity into the by now mature organization.

The challenge is therefore to maintain a **healthy balance** in the company's behaviour patterns as it develops – to introduce more repetitive behaviour early on, and to introduce more adaptation at a later stage. This may sound easy. It is not. The balanced position is in fact an **unstable equilibrium**. It requires nurturing two diametrically opposed behavioural styles side-by-side within the organization. This requires continuous management attention – otherwise one of the two opposing behavioural traits will take over. The company will revert to being either repetitive or adaptive (Figure 34).

Figure 34: The optimal balanced position is an unstable equilibrium: organizations naturally regress to being either adaptive or repetitive in nature.

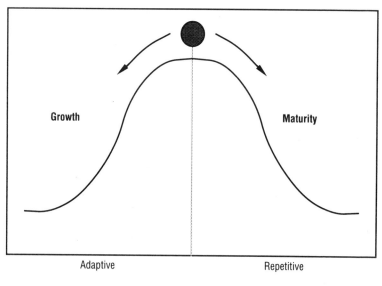

Growth

Maturity

Adaptive

Repetitive

Behaviour patterns

Maintaining the right balance can lead to tremendous success:

■ *3M manages to foster an environment which supports adaptation and innovation. It produces a constant stream of new products. Individual managers are encouraged to develop new ideas and product concepts – provided they fulfil their ongoing responsibilities. The organization tolerates managers spending up to a quarter of their time on their own pet projects. At the same time 3M ruthlessly exploits the strengths of its established core businesses, such as Scotch Tape.*

■ *Kwik-Fit is highly repetitive in its core business: individual outlets are run with engineering-like precision. Every operation is timed and costed with meticulous care. In parallel with this tight focus on the base business, the top management group have been highly adaptive. They have managed to test and introduce a growing range of additional services. Several of these have now been rolled out to form separate chains.*

Conversely, firms which diverge too far to either side of the balanced position normally suffer:

■ *People Express was initially highly focused. It lost its strategic direction acquiring Frontier. From being a focused, low cost competitor it suddenly tried to be all things to all men. The company lost its distinctive positioning in the market. Its costs crept upwards. Shortly afterwards it was taken over by Texas Air. The firm had become too adaptive.*

■ *Volkswagen's excessive focus on the Beetle nearly sunk the firm. By adapting and coming up with the Golf, it saved the day.*

An alternative to maintaining a balance is to oscillate between the two extremes. Periods of adaptive behaviour are followed by a switch to more repetitive patterns and so on. During the adaptive periods the firm is generating lots of ideas and opportunities, searching for a new direction. As it makes the transition to a repetitive style it chooses the direction and focuses on it. This is pursued with success until it needs to reassess its direction once again, whereupon it reverts to being adaptive. Needless to say, these transitions can be highly traumatic times.

Professor Birch of MIT suggested this as his 'pulsation model' of how successful firms develop. Progress is rarely steady. Periods of dramatic growth are followed by times of crisis, before the company grows once more. These mark the transitions between different behavioural styles (Figure 35).

MANAGING THE BALANCE

What can senior management do to achieve the optimal balance between the adaptive and repetitive skills in their companies? This issue transcends innovation itself. It is a fundamental question of the firm's strategy, culture, people and organization structure. It is not immediately amenable to quantitative analysis. We are dealing here with

Figure 35: The Pulsation Model of company growth

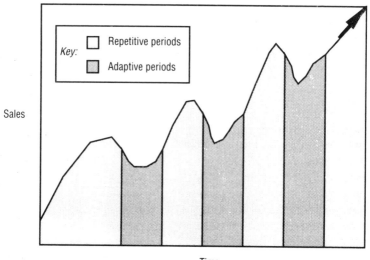

shades of grey, rather than black and white. Instead of making strategic choices simpler, however, it makes them all the more difficult: with few hard and fast rules to go by, it is only too easy to drift into platitudes and clichéd solutions. The issue can be addressed at two levels:

- **General guidelines:** as a general rule, young innovative companies tend to be too adaptive. Successful mature firms, on the other hand, tend to be overly repetitive in their behaviour. Needless to say, exceptions abound. For many companies, however, the imbalance will be quite clear. If management can reach an internal consensus on this, then they have completed the critical first step in solving the problem. The broad directions in which the firm must move can be agreed and acted upon.

- **Explicit debate:** in many situations, however, general guidelines such as those above are inadequate. There can be significant uncertainty and debate as to whether the firm is too adaptive or too repetitive in its approach. Are our problems caused by insufficient focus and concentration of resources on our major opportunities? Or should we be casting the net wider and considering broader options? Are the declining returns in our core business the result of inadequate attention being given to it, or are we over-investing already?

The behavioural review

Resolving questions like these requires an objective methodology. A behavioural review process is needed which can help provide both the quality of decision and the level of proof which management requires before it can commit to major and fundamental changes of direction.

By itself the review cannot produce concrete prescriptions. There are no right or wrong answers: different companies can approach a given business situation in very different ways with equal success. The approach which works for one may be entirely inappropriate for another. It is perhaps this lack of clear-cut answers which deters most companies from fully addressing the behavioural issues they face. They assume that their existing approach is the right one for them, even though it has normally arisen in a more or less arbitrary way. Perhaps the fundamental point is worth repeating: too many companies fail to reach their full potential because they have inappropriate behaviour patterns. In essence what a behavioural review can achieve is quite straightforward:

- It can **raise the level of debate** by providing objective inputs on this very fuzzy subject. With this information in place, top management can begin to choose the direction and make the right changes happen.

All of this may sound like a major exercise causing an additional workload for the small innovative company. This need not be the case. What is required above all is an objective, intellectually honest appraisal of the firm, its environment and its people. While in a mature firm this will call for some specific information gathering and analysis, in a small one it can be conveniently integrated into management's overall planning process. It need not take much time. The results, however, can be startling. By explicitly discussing the behavioural issue, management is opening up the debate in a critical area which few firms ever address. Starting this debate is the first step in moving towards a position where the firm's behavioural style can be positively managed. It gives the company a rare and valuable competitive advantage.

The review consists of some straightforward analyses of the firm and its operations. Some are quantitative, others qualitative. Some are independent variables, directly under management's control, while others are dependent variables, the results of actions taken elsewhere. Together they can give a clear picture of how the firm is behaving. The main measures are:

- Novelty ratios
- Segmentation
- Rollout vs hedge
- Margin trends
- Overhead trends
- Experience curves
- Return on investment
- Organizational stress.

- **Novelty ratios:** Adaptive firms are, by definition, constantly changing. They have high novelty. Toffler developed his novelty ratio to measure this. One simply calculates the proportion of all sales which are accounted for by products which have been introduced in the last one year/three years/five years. The higher the novelty ratio, the more adaptive the firm is (Figure 36).

Figure 36: Novelty ratios help show how adaptive the firm is.

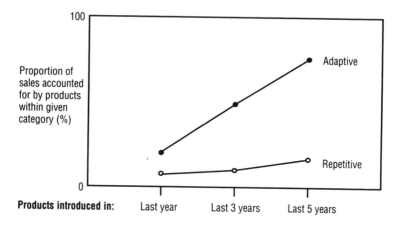

The product dimension is only one aspect of novelty, however. There are many other ways in which firms can be adaptive, such as:

- Product ranges
- Product variants, within existing ranges
- Customer segments
- Individual customers

- Distribution channels
- Geographic areas
- Technologies.

Individually these measures say a lot about both how adaptive the firm has been, and in which dimensions it has been adaptive. In combination they are even more revealing. Some firms adapt significantly, but along only one or two dimensions – e.g. they adapt by reaching new customer segments through new distribution channels, but do this with a familiar technology and product. Others try to adapt along several dimensions at once. They simultaneously change all elements of the marketing mix. Occasionally this works. When it does, it can result in radical and dramatically successful innovations:

- *Benetton, for example, innovated in almost all key areas of its business system: manufacturing methods, product design, retail outlets, management systems. The results have been impressive: the firm has rapidly established a unique position in fashion retailing worldwide.*

More commonly, however, being adaptive and attempting innovation in several areas at once is less successful. It introduces too much complexity into the organization. There are too many changing variables, too much to go wrong.

- **Segmentation:** one of the clearest and most significant trends in business today is to segment markets ever more finely. Evolution of customer needs and changes in the supply economics of many industries are continually opening up new opportunities for niche players. Identifying and pursuing new segmentation opportunities is one powerful way in which adaptive firms can compete.

  How many different segments does the firm target today, and approach with a distinct product/service offering? Two years ago? Five years ago? Have completely new segments been addressed? Have existing businesses been resegmented?

- **Rollout vs hedge:** how does the firm develop its new ideas and businesses? According to a carefully planned strategy, in which specific markets and customer groups are attacked first, before successively moving on to others (the rollout)? Or in a more haphazard fashion, with several opportunities being pursued in parallel so that none are left unexploited (the hedge)? The most adaptive firms tend to follow up all the interesting leads they get, spreading their efforts across many areas. More repetitive ones tend to focus more tightly.

Does the firm say 'no' to any opportunities? If so, to what proportion? Many adaptive companies seem almost incapable of doing so. They follow up every lead, even if only at a low level of effort. It all creates added complexity, however, as the firm dissipates its efforts in pursuing several opportunities in parallel.

What resources are expended on what could loosely be termed 'new ventures'? How many such ventures are there? What proportion of resources are spent on the most significant one? The most significant five? Ten? The more adaptive the firm, the more fragmented its efforts will tend to be. Occasionally this can be successful. More often, it severely limits the progress made in any one area.

The cash flow profiles of new ventures have a story to tell. They tend to be negative at first, as the firm needs to build up the opportunity into a strong business. Later development is more revealing. Highly adaptive firms rarely settle on a coherent strategy for long: they keep exploring new avenues instead of exploiting any one opportunity to the full. Consequently, none is invested in with the fullest commitment. Rarely do any develop into major generators of cash. The firm's portfolio consists of a large number of individual businesses and ventures, the vast majority of which will be close to cash neutral: few will either generate or use large amounts of cash.

The repetitive firm is completely different. It focuses on a few core businesses. Some of these will typically be well established and have strong competitive positions. They generate large amounts of cash. Others are still being invested in, generally with a high degree of focus and commitment. The resulting portfolio consists of relatively few businesses, some of which have strong positive cash flows, others negative. The common failing of the repetitive firm is not so much that it lacks cash cows, but rather that it has few new ventures in which to invest its cash. It lacks excitement and dynamism.

- **Margin trends:** differ between adaptive and repetitive firms. Most new ventures earn high gross margins early on, but these tend to decline as the market matures and becomes more competitive. Market niches and customers' special requirements typically support higher gross margins than the mass market.

  Adaptive firms therefore tend to enjoy high gross margins over a period of time. Their mix of business has new ventures and high margin niches. Conversely, repetitive firms' gross margins are generally lower and tend to decline over time as the firm focuses increasingly on maturing businesses.

- **Overheads:** behave similarly to the margin situation. Adaptation leads to high overhead levels in two distinct ways: firstly, new ventures typically incur greater overhead burdens than mature ones and, secondly, the sheer diversity of most adaptive firms brings with it the overheads that are always associated with complexity. Repetitive firms tend to have lower overhead levels, which decline as the firm's products mature (Figure 37).

Figure 37: Gross margins and overheads behave differently for repetitive and adaptive firms

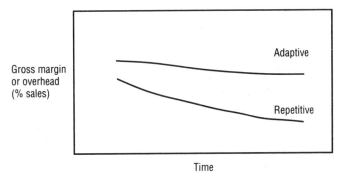

- **Experience curves:** can also display differences between adaptive and repetitive firms. The real unit cost of a product or service is plotted against the total accumulated volume produced since production began. Typically, costs decline by a constant proportion each time volume doubles.

Firms which are strongly committed to one product and focus tightly on it tend to grow in volume rapidly and exploit all available cost reduction possibilities. They move quickly down their experience curves. Conversely, those which pursue every opportunity they come across are forever changing the specification of the product. They seldom keep doing one thing for long enough to build up any significant experience base. Their experience curves tend to be less steep, and they progress down them less rapidly. Costs do not decline as quickly as for the repetitive firm.

- **Return on investment:** every firm's core business presents opportunities for investment. The number and type of investment made tells a lot about the firm. Repetitive firms tend to invest heavily in their base businesses, with numerous projects aimed at cost reduction, efficiency improvement etc. If anything, they tend to over-invest in their cores, with the marginal investment producing returns below the true (risk-adjusted) cost of capital. Plotting the investments which have been made over a number of years, together with the return on those investments, shows a characteristic picture (Figure 38). Some investments show good returns, but there are several which actually earn less than the cost of capital. Shareholders would have been better off if these latter investments had not been made: the firm has over-invested in its core business.

  Adaptive firms typically make far fewer investments in their core businesses: most effort is being expended on exciting opportunities elsewhere. The investments which are made in the core business typically earn good returns (being the most obviously attractive investments to make in the core). These firms are, however, missing further attractive opportunities in their core. The rate of return on the marginal investment is usually well above the cost of capital. Several quite attractive investment opportunities in the base business have probably been missed. The best balance usually lies somewhere between the adaptive and repetitive extremes.

Figure 38: Repetitive firms normally over-invest in their core businesses, while adaptive firms under-invest.

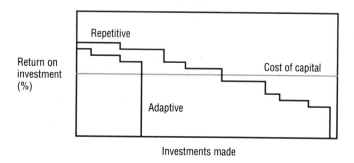

- **Organizational stress:** certain individuals and groups do indeed thrive on uncertainty and excitement. In the most adaptive of organizations, however, the strains begin to show. There comes a point where excessive fragmentation of responsibilities can cease to provide a challenge and instead merely limit management's efficiency and effectiveness. Job definitions and responsibilities are usually vague; so are reporting relationships and other procedures. The situation in repetitive organizations is precisely the reverse: roles and responsibilities are usually carefully laid out, and performance monitored. The principal challenge for senior management is often how to inject some excitement and stress into the organization.

The end result of both extremes can be similar: reduced productivity, dissatisfaction and increasing staff turnover. The remedies, however, are drastically different. Understanding the root causes of organizational stress is a prerequisite for corrective action.

The review is the first step in enabling management to influence behavioural styles within the company. It puts the whole process on a more objective, quantifiable basis than is normally the case. By so doing, it raises the level of discussion, bringing out into the open complex issues which are normally left unexplored or taken for granted. Few firms do this: the review can provide unique and valuable insights.

Implementing the changes required, which lies beyond the scope of this book, lies at the very heart of the responsibilities of senior management. The review does, however, provide answers to several important questions. Should we be more selective about pursuing new opportunities? More imaginative? Should we invest more in the core business? Less? Do we take sufficient care in setting and implementing strategy? Is the organization too fluid? Top management can make some of the necessary changes directly. Rigorous investment appraisal and approval procedures can be introduced to gain control over a too-adaptive programme of new ventures. Strategic planning programmes can be introduced to enforce a more systematic approach to the business. Task forces can be set up to investigate investment opportunities in the company's core businesses. Changes in company culture take longer to effect, but they start to come about as top management are seen to commit themselves to the more direct changes.

Attaining the right behavioural balance is critical to any firm's success. It is the medium that translates opportunities into realities. Too much adaptation and its innovations will not realize their full cash-generating potential. Behavioural style must be managed.

SUMMARY

Innovation in a narrow sense is insufficient to guarantee superior financial performance.

- **Broad perspective** is required: innovative concepts have to be effectively translated into strong cash generators.

Companies display characteristic behaviour patterns:

- **Adaptive**
- **Repetitive**

The mix between these typically changes as the firm evolves from birth to maturity.

Achieving the **right balance** between adaptive and repetitive behaviour is critical to success.

- Difficult to achieve: **unstable equilibrium.**

Management can actively influence the balance within the firm.

- The **behavioural review** is one important tool for this.

INDEX